MANINBO: PEACE & WAR

고은 **KO UN**

MANINBO
PEACE & WAR

TRANSLATED BY
BROTHER ANTHONY OF TAIZÉ & LEE SANG-WHA

BLOODAXE BOOKS

Copyright © Ko Un 2015
Translations & introductory material
© Brother Anthony of Taizé & Lee Sang-Wha 2015

ISBN: 978 1 78037 242 6

First published 2015 by
Bloodaxe Books Ltd,
Eastburn,
South Park,
Hexham,
Northumberland NE46 1BS.

www.bloodaxebooks.com
For further information about Bloodaxe titles
please visit our website or write to
the above address for a catalogue.

Supported using public funding by
ARTS COUNCIL
ENGLAND

THE DAISAN FOUNDATION

Thanks are due to The Daisan Foundation for financial support
relating to the translation and publication costs of this book.

Cover design: Neil Astley & Pamela Robertson-Pearce.

Printed in Great Britain by Bell & Bain Limited, Glasgow, Scotland, on
acid-free paper sourced from mills with FSC chain of custody certification.

ACKNOWLEDGEMENTS

Five of these poems were published in Volume 1 (2007) of *Azalea* (published by Harvard University's Center of Korean Studies) and have been slightly revised since: 'Eonnyeon in Siberia', 'Hallelujah', 'Yi Jeong-yi's Family', 'DDT' and 'Gweon Jin-gyu'. Six of the poems appeared in *The Hundred Years' War: modern war poems*, edited by Neil Astley (Bloodaxe Books, 2014).

CONTENTS

For the Faces of the World

The reason why there is night should be the stars. Beneath the starlight of the night sky I have lived the chronology of my poetry.

In October 1979 I provided one of the motivations for an incident by which the most blatant dictatorship in modern Korean history had to be brought to an end. After the assassination of the dictator, I was freed from prison. However, in May the following year, with the second military coup, I abruptly became a criminal, guilty of conspiring to rebel, violating martial law, and inciting others to violate martial law, etc.

The special cell in the military prison was a closed space without windows, measuring 1.5 metres by 1 metre. Given the state of emergency in force then, my very survival was most uncertain. I had already decided what my final gesture would be when the time came for me to die. Deprived of present time in that despair, the incompetent act of remembering alone served as a substitute for the present time. I began to realise that remembering and imagining something could be a source of strength, enabling me to endure day by day the darkness and the fear.

The works that I would have to write if I survived and went back to the world were born in that way. Those were the seeds for the seven-volume epic *Mount Baekdu* and the thirty-volume *Maninbo* (Ten Thousand Lives). Thanks to campaigns inside Korea and abroad, I came back out into the world a few years later. Marrying belatedly at fifty, I began life with my wife. This married life has been a time filling my epic and lyrical works with the sound of the waves of the ocean.

I don't think that the active volcano of my poetic passion that once again began to erupt was a destiny allotted to me only. It was a blessing descending to me through the blood of all the sounds of birds and animals living in the primeval forests of the tropical regions on the Pacific equator as well as of the lengthy oral narratives, lasting several days, that were transmitted in the Eurasian continent since prehistoric times.

Maninbo is a collection of songs about the people I have come to know in this world. The encounters I have had are no private matter, but essentially public. This public nature cannot vanish by

13

our personal forgetfulness or neglect. It is the commemoration of the truth of life itself, resisting ephemeral nature. Even one of our trivial meetings has an integrality of history contained within it. I took that as a principle, so I tried to depict not only people's noble aspects but also their ugly ones.

Maninbo begins with portraits of the villagers of my home town from my childhood in the 1930s. And the central five volumes, from volume 16 to volume 20, are filled with random, fragmentary portraits evoking the several millions who died during the three years of the Korean War from 1950, as well as those who survived amidst the ruins of war.

I did not try to portray only people. It was because human beings cannot exist without the 'mandala' of this world. Part of my task was to manifest the world. I finished *Maninbo* with thirty volumes, in which some 4,000 people come on the stage from all walks of life, from our country's history and land. That also includes those whom I met in my years of wandering and those who appeared briefly at turning points in Korea's history.

Maninbo is both my poetic study of people and my nameless historic act. For a poet cannot live without the organic function of history. Having completed this project, I truly had the feeling that I had made the past lives of those people whom I met or whom I did not meet present, one by one, either in reality or in history. This is also a realisation of the mourning that has been one of the topics of my writing.

While I was writing *Maninbo* I strove to overcome to some degree the poetic first-person. Frame is sometimes fatal. The poet opens his eyes in the grey of today's morning leaving the light of the previous day behind. In recent years I have raised questions regarding the poetic speaking voice: how I could bring multiple poetic, metaphorical selves to life through the first-person 'I' in a poem, how I could attain the truth of each one of endless others, for how long 'I' could remain me, with no end.

The view that wouldn't take poetry as anything more than a kind of fantasy existed already in ancient times and Lukács also expressed it. Even without that, I was sure that I did not want to defend for ever the identity of the speaker in a poem.

If the modern age is the age of the self, then according to this ostentatious common sense modern poetry is a poetry that realises the self. The 'I' as the subject in modern poetry is accepted as an almost absolute condition. The 'I' in poetry is something like an event as moving as when four-legged animals first became two-legged humans and stood on the ground. The world becomes different for the first time with that.

However, the modern self might never be a gift that we could receive easily. The path leading to the self is incomparably challenging. The ideology of God, the ideology of the group repressed for long outpourings of the self. History has shown a violence that tramples down the potential of the self.

In the time of the feudal ages of North-East Asia, Korea designated the majority of the subjugated classes as nameless objects. In such regions, the self was bound to appear either as a threat or an unexpected force, or too late. The period of division following the Japanese colonial period was also much more of an adversity to the self. 'I' barely survived by killing 'I'. Apart from these adversities, 'I' have not dropped anchor until today, with an acute recognition that there is no way to seek for the self.

The 'I' in modern Korean poetry has these hard times as wounds. But when such an 'I' becomes stuck in the barbarous egocentrism of modernity, if another self that can take it out does not appear, we would have a reality of double pain.

The speaking 'I' is an illusion if it does not have the 'exterior' of mind, that constitutes a necessary prerequisite for the imagining of a narrative structure about people and the world and human self-discovery. Statements about reality and the portrayal of society and humanity would be reduced to a dried-up river-bed if there were no memoir of imagination. Here I dream of a new third-person narrator. Now the third-person is not something matching the absolute first and second-person, but signifies the inner dialectic of those.

When we ponder whether modernity is a creative age that has liberated the self, when there is almost no ground for claiming that modernity is not a chronicle that has exercised a violence of control repressing the self, then we come to realise how wounded the modern self is. Therefore, we have to seek 'a new other of the self' by re-modernising the modern and reflecting on the modern self. In this respect, the flash of a poet who said that our soul is a dream for others is still vibrating. 'I' am reborn in another's dream.

15

It is certain that all the interiority of poetry will breathe anew so long as poetry has a yearning for the exterior that is the source of poetry. The self is a complex body that has an exterior as an expansion of the self and an interior as a interlocking of the self. It is therefore no empty words to say that all the world resides in a mote of dust. Penetrating into the world! We can explain this as: when the self becomes other, that is another self and from there a new self as another is born, then the speaker in a poem will return to ultimate selflessness. I cannot exist without you, without a committed devotion to you, and ultimately 'I' become not only you but the third-person Indra's Net that is an infinite plural of 'I' and 'you' and attain an emptiness that is neither private nor public. That emptiness is the Buddhist 'being in profundity'. The speaking 'I' is the world of an 'other I.'

The world of *Maninbo* is a world where unfamiliar relationships evolve between the poet, the speaking voice, and the subject being depicted or the action existing between the lines. An interpretation of human beings is possible in the process in which they establish inseparable, irreversible relationships. It is the never-ending life where you are I, I am you, and you are he or someone and that someone is another I ... the movement of the world. The stage for the social cycle which begets the freedom of 'I' and others is the space of *Maninbo*. I, the author, cannot but be an alter ego of that 'I'. Society is like that. Therefore, the distinction between good and evil, beautiful and ugly can be valid only when we get rid of the logic of one domination. Dream produces a cyclical ethics, like a snake biting its own tail.

Many years ago, a volume of English translations of poems selected from volumes 1 through 10 of *Maninbo* was published in the US. The present volume contains poems selected from volumes 11 through 20. The subjects of many of the poems in this volume are obtained from the traces of my experiences prior to and during the 1950s. They depict tragic scenes – situations of life and imminent death, the things that happened when traditional society collapsed, existence and ruins, incursion of ideology, migrations of population, a war that caused dehumanisation, and the possibility of humanity in that war. The ruins gave birth to what follows despair.

The portraits of Korean people gain universality in that they are not only portraits of Koreans but the portraits of human beings.

My dream is that this volume, including poems that contain the situations and truth of an atrocious period on the Korean peninsula, will serve to offer the opportunity for us to reflect on the human world where wars have never ceased.

Uisang, the great Korean monk of ancient times, spread all over the Korean peninsula the Buddhist Huayan notion that 'All is one, one is all'. 1500 years after him, my mind too opens its arms wide toward the fetal movement of a mote of dust and, on the largest scale, the grandiose action of the expansion of the universe.

KO UN

Translators' Preface

Maninbo (Ten Thousand Lives) is the title of a remarkable collection of poems by Ko Un, filling thirty volumes, a total of four thousand and one poems containing the names of 5600 people, which took 30 years to complete. Ko Un first conceived the idea while confined in a solitary cell upon his arrest in May 1980, the first volumes appeared in 1986, and the project was completed 25 years after publication began, in 2010. Robert Hass, former American Poet Laureate, who has also written a long essay on *Maninbo*, remarked on the completion of the huge project in 2010, 'That poem, or the part of it that has moved and excited readers of the English translation, is a gift to the world, a stunning portrait of the 20th century in all its humanity and violence, and a tribute to the vitality of the Korean people.' It is certainly hard to think of any other contemporary poet's work which can rival *Maninbo* in its complexity, its sheer vitality, and its ability to cover so many aspects of a nation's history. It becomes even more amazing when we remember the eighty other volumes of poetry and prose Ko Un published in the years during which he was working on *Maninbo*.

An earlier volume of translations in English published in the United States in 2005 contained some 160 poems from volumes 1 to 10 of *Maninbo*. This present volume contains poems from volumes 11 to 20. We hope that a third volume will offer poems from the last ten volumes.

The last half of this volume is selected from volumes 16 to 20 of *Maninbo*, which is focused on the sufferings of the Korean people during the Korean War. We have made our selections with consideration of how ordinary people suffer from warfare in a world that has, in recent times, never known a period without war. We have also considered what might be most accessible to readers unfamiliar with the events of Korean history.

Ko Un first conceived the *Maninbo* project while he was in prison after the military coup of May 1980. Languishing in solitary confinement in a military prison, unsure whether he might be executed or not, he found his mind filling with memories of the people he had met or heard of during his life. Finally, he made a vow that, if he was released from prison, he would write poems about each of them. In part this would be a means of rescuing from oblivion countless lives that would otherwise be lost, and also it would serve to offer a vision of the history of Korea as it has been lived by its entire population through the centuries. The poems are written in a particular style, created by Ko Un and named by him 'popular-historical poetry'. Essentially narrative, each poem offers a brief glimpse of an individual's life. Some span an entire existence, some relate a brief moment. Some are celebrations of remarkable lives, others recall terrible events and inhuman beings. Some poems are humorous, others are dark commemorations of unthinkable incidents. They span the whole of Korean history, from earliest pre-history to the present time.

We have tried to preserve the specific flavour of the Korean poems, which are free in structure, brief evocations, divided often into short sections, with snatches of dialogue, glimpses of events. We are very grateful to the American poet Hillel Schwartz for reading our translations and making insightful suggestions for poetic improvement. We have avoided overloading the poems with explanatory notes and assume that readers will consult a map of Korea if they wish to identify the many places named in the poems. The history of Korea, like its geography, is not well-known in the world at large. We hope that this collection will help many discover the tragic yet intensely human lives that so many Koreans have led, simply, nobly, often with immense dignity amidst a painful reality.

BROTHER ANTHONY OF TAIZÉ
& LEE SANG-WHA

A Brief Summary of Korean History

These poems contain so many references to Korean history, ancient and modern, that the reader will soon be looking for help. Explanations are best done in a separate general summary, rather than by multiple notes to individual poems.

Ancient Korea: Goguryeo, Baekje, Silla, and Goryeo

Korea is today divided into South and North Korea, officially designated as the Republic of Korea and the Democratic People's Republic of Korea, respectively. Together, they occupy the entire Korean Peninsula. This division is recent, the fruit of the Korean War. Historically, we find the peninsula divided into a number of distinct kingdoms at the start of the present era, but for many centuries the whole peninsula was a single nation. In the northernmost part, originally centred in and reaching far into what was later known as Manchuria, was Goguryeo. That kingdom, recorded as having been established in 37 BC, lasted as an independent entity until 669.

The southern border of Goguryeo slowly moved southward down the peninsula until it reached the region now occupied by Seoul. The western portion of southern Korea was governed by the kingdom known as Baekje, founded in 18 BC and independent until 660. Further south, the south-east portion of the peninsula was occupied by Silla, with its capital in the city now known as Gyeongju, where the dynasty was founded in 57 BC and continued as a kingdom until 918, starting as a local kingdom, then becoming an enlarged 'Unified Silla' integrating the Gaya kingdom in 532, Baekje in 660, and then Goguryeo in 668 with the military support of Tang China.

After a long period of dynastic decline, the royal dynasty of Silla was toppled and a new dynasty arose, known as Goryeo, established in 918 and lasting until 1392, with its main capital much further to the north, for much of the time in Gaeseong, to the north of what is now Seoul. Buddhism had entered all parts of Korea well before the Silla unification. It formed a very strong feature in the culture of Goryeo, when temples became rich and powerful while individual monks exercised great influence at court.

Finally, just as Ming China was emerging after the end of the Mongol domination, Korean court politics led to the overturn of the reigning dynasty of Goryeo and a new dynasty was proclaimed in 1392, with the name Joseon. The new royal family bore the family name Yi. The kingdom of Joseon, or the Joseon era, lasted until 1897, during which time it remained in a tribute-relationship with the Chinese emperor. The capital city was relocated to the town of Hanyang, which was renamed 'Seoul' (meaning 'Capital city'). The Joseon era was marked by a strong reaction against Buddhism and an equally strong emphasis on a rigid form of Confucianism. Many hundreds of temples were destroyed, monks were not allowed to enter Seoul, and those temples that survived were mostly located in remote rural areas.

Near the start of the Joseon era, under the reign of King Sejong, the Korean alphabet ('hangeul') was invented to allow easy writing of the multiple syllables of Korean grammar, as well as those Korean words which did not correspond to any Chinese character. The written language of education and administration was Classical Chinese and the high-class scholars saw no need for this new invention. It was branded 'women's writing' and only came into its own with the beginning of modernity late in the 19th century.

The greatest crisis during the Joseon era was the Japanese invasion that began in 1592. That year was known in Korea as Imjin year and therefore the entire invasion is often known as the Imjin Wars. The invasion was launched by Toyotomi Hideyoshi with the aim of crossing Korea, marching into China and conquering it. He had wrongly assumed that the Koreans would offer no resistance. When Korea asserted its loyalty to China, and thwarted the Japanese plan, the Japanese armies turned against Korea and systematically set about burning it. Almost every significant building in Korea was destroyed in the years that followed. China belatedly sent forces to support Korea and finally, with the death of Hideyoshi in 1598, the Japanese withdrew.

In the following century, the Manchus established the Qing dynasty in China in 1644. Joseon felt a strong loyalty to Ming China on account of the help they had provided against the Japanese. Therefore they opposed the Manchu and this led to two Manchu invasions of Joseon, in 1627 and again in 1637, ending in humiliating defeat for the Koreans. Late Joseon was marked by intense rivalry between different court factions, which led at times to violent purges and multiple exiles. The Joseon era was marked by a fierce resistance to all contact with the rest of the world, beyond strictly controlled relations with China and Japan.

Early Modern Korea

Modern history in the Far East began on 3 January 1868, when the new Emperor of Japan made a formal declaration of the restoration of his power. This was the beginning of the Meiji Reforms, by which Japan emerged from isolation and became part of the modern world. Japan soon awakened to the possibility that it, too, might establish an empire and a first step would be to gain control of Korea. The Ganghwa Treaty between Japan and Joseon was signed on 26 February 1876. The United States and the other major western powers were not far behind.

Japan had already determined to take control of the Korean peninsula, stationing armed forces and police there, and in 1896 a group of Japanese thugs murdered the Korean Queen, Queen Min, for opposing the Japanese plans. In the decade that followed, Japan ruthlessly robbed Korea of its independence and forced Gojong, the king of Joseon, off the throne when he tried to resist. In 1910 Joseon was formally annexed by Japan. For the following decades Chosen was the name of a colonised Japanese province, where all education and administration used uniquely the Japanese language and where Korean culture was treated with disdain. Thousands of Koreans, reduced to penury, either fled to Manchuria or went to seek work in Japan.

On 1 March 1919, exasperated by years of intense Japanese repression, the Korean population staged street demonstrations demanding independence, the March 1 Independence Movement. After this, a Provisional Government in Exile was established in Shanghai and later groups of militant independence fighters would fight guerrilla campaigns against the Japanese in Manchuria and Siberia.

Then came the Pacific War, which ended on 15 August 1945, with the surrender of Japan. One condition of the act of surrender was that Japan would withdraw from all occupied territories, including Korea, so this date is known in Korea as 'Liberation'. A few weeks before this, at a meeting of the allied leaders in Cairo, the United States had proposed and the Soviet Union agreed that after the defeat of Japan, Korea would be occupied by the US and the USSR, each taking responsibility for half the peninsula, defined by the 38th parallel running just north of Seoul.

The Americans brought with them a Korean exile who had long lived in the US, Yi Seung-man, known in the West as Dr Syngman Rhee. Meanwhile, many Koreans across southern Korea believed that they had now gained the freedom to run their country for themselves as they thought best, following more or less socialistic models. They were very soon branded 'Communists' ('Palgaengi' or 'reds') by supporters of Syngman Rhee and the American Military Government. Some took to the hills as guerrillas. The result was a reign of terror in which countless innocent folk were massacred as 'reds'. One of the most notorious and atrocious mass-acres happened in Jeju Island on 3 April 1948, when thousands of innocent civilians, including children, were killed.

Meanwhile, in the northern half of the peninsula, the USSR quickly handed control to the local Communist Party with the support of many guerrila fighters returning from Manchuria and Siberia. Hundreds of Christians and landowners began to flee southward, while many of Korea's brightest intellectuals and writers rejoiced in the establishment of a socialist regime in the North and were glad to go there to support it. As a result of the growth of the Cold War, in 1948 two opposing republics of Korea, South and North, were proclaimed, each claiming to control the entire Korean peninsula.

The Korean War

On 25 June 1950, the North Korean army (Korean People's Army, KPA) began to advance southward across the 38th parallel. This act of aggression or invasion was brought to the attention of the United Nations Security Council, which the USSR was then boy-cotting, and after debating the matter, the Security Council recom-mended that member states provide military assistance to the Rep-ublic of Korea.

As they launched their first attack, the North Koreans had a combined force that included tanks supported by heavy artillery; the South Koreans, lacking tanks, anti-tank weapons, or heavy artillery, could not stop such an attack. On 27 June, Syngman Rhee evacuated secretly from Seoul with some of the government. The next day the South Korean Army blew up the only bridge across the Han River in an attempt to stop the North Korean army. The bridge was blown up without warning while 4,000 refugees were crossing it, and hundreds were killed. Seoul fell to North Korea that same day.

By August, the allies controlled only a small area in the vicinity of Pusan, in south-east Korea. The rest of the country was declared part of the North Korean 'People's Republic'. General MacArthur landed a large force at Incheon, on the west coast, on 15 September 1950. On 25 September, Seoul was recaptured and the North Koreans soon began to retreat northwards.

By 1 October 1950, the North Koreans had withdrawn past the 38th parallel; the UN forces followed them northwards, meeting minimal resitance, and soon the allied forces had reached the Chinese border. The Chinese decided to intervene. After secretly crossing the Yalu River on 19 October, the Chinese People's Volunteer Army (PVA) launched their first offensive, attacking the advancing UN forces near the border. The UN forces began to retreat and were forced back below the 38th parallel border in mid December.

On New Year's Eve of 1950, the Chinese launched a new offensive into South Korea, which overwhelmed the UN forces, allowing the PVA and KPA on 4 January 1951 to conquer Seoul for the second time. The withdrawal of the allied forces together with most of the population from Seoul is known as the 'January Retreat'. Two months later, the PVA and the KPA were again dislodged from Seoul (14 March 1951) and by the end of May, the allies had established the so-called 'Line Kansas' just north of the 38th parallel. Then began a stalemate that lasted until the Armistice of 1953. The 'Line Kansas' (or Kansas Line) was to form the basis for the present frontier between the two Koreas.

Armistice negotiations began 10 July 1951 at Kaesong. They continued for two years, first at Kaesong, afterwards relocated at Panmunjom. The final armistice agreement was signed on 27 July 1953, by the UN Command, China and North Korea. The Republic of Korea did not sign. The two Koreas were to be separated by a demilitarised zone (DMZ). Prisoners of war not wishing to be returned to their home countries were allowed to ask to be sent to a neutral third country.

After the War: The April Revolution and Park Jung-hee

Syngman Rhee remained as president at the head of an increasingly corrupt regime, desperately holding onto power by all means. Finally, the citizens began to protest, provoked by blatantly falsified election results early in 1960. On 19 April 1960 thousands of university students and high school students marched on the Blue House, the presidential mansion, demanding new elections and calling for Rhee's resignation, their numbers growing to over 100,000. Police opened fire on the protestors, killing approximately 180 and wounding thousands. On 26 April, President Rhee stepped down from power and went into voluntary exile. This series of events is known as the 'April Revolution'.

South Korea adopted a parliamentary system which considerably weakened the power of the president and so, while Yun Bo-seon was elected President on 13 August 1960, real power was vested in the prime minister. Following months of political instability, on 19 May 1961 Lt General Park Chung-hee launched a coup d'état overthrowing the short-lived Second Republic of South Korea and replacing it with a military junta and later the autocratic Third Republic of South Korea. Almost at once, he authorised the establishment in 1961 of the Korean Central Intelligence Agency (KCIA). This was the notorious office responsible for the repression of political and social dissent throughout his time in power, and beyond. After Yun resigned in 1962, Lt General Park consolidated his power by becoming acting president. In 1963, he was elected president in his own right. In 1971, Park won another close election against his rival, Kim Dae-jung. Shortly after being sworn in, he declared a state of emergency, and in October 1972, Park dissolved the legislature and suspended the 1963 constitution. The so-called Yushin ('revitalising') Constitution was approved in a heavily-rigged plebiscite in November 1972.

Meanwhile, South Korea had begun the processes of industrialisation and urbanisation that were to catapult it to its current position in the world. This was done at the expense of many basic human rights, with low wages, absence of trade unions, arbitrary arrests and random killings. Finally, as more and more people were taking to the streets to demand a return to democracy and a liberalisation of society, Park seemed to be preparing a violent crackdown when he was assassinated by Kim Jae-gyu, the head of the Korean Central Intelligence Agency, on 26 October, 1979.

For a while, it seemed that the dreamed-of restoration of democracy might happen, but on 18 May 1980, General Chun Doo-hwan staged a coup while provoking an uprising in the south-western city of Gwangju which left hundreds dead. All the leading dissidents, including Ko Un, were thrown into prison and a new dictatorship began...

After continuing resistance and sacrifice on the part of many dissidents, climaxing in huge demonstrations in June 1987 which forced the dictatorial regime to accept a democratic Constitution, Korea was finally able to elect a civilian president in 1992. Since then, in spite of ongoing ideological conflicts between Left and Right, Korea has continued to develop her democratic system, while becoming one of the world's leading economic powers.

Ko Un: A Short Biography

Ko Un was born in 1933 in Gunsan, North Jeolla Province, South Korea. He made his official debut as a poet in 1958 while a Buddhist monk. For a decade he practiced Seon meditation and travelled throughout the country.

After returning to the secular world in 1962, he hurled himself into a nihilism full of desperation and alcohol, producing many striking works. He was awakened to the social reality of his country by the self-immolation of a poor labourer, Jeon Tae-il, late in 1970 and became engaged in political and social issues, opposing the military regime and joining the struggle for human rights and the labour movement.

For more than a decade, he was, many times and for long periods, persecuted by the Korean CIA, with arrests, house arrests, detentions, tortures and imprisonments. In 1980 he was sentenced to 20 years' imprisonment, but thanks to international efforts he was set free with a general pardon in 1982, after serving two and a half ' years' imprisonment in solitary confinement.

He married at the age of 50, and then followed a period of productivity unparalleled in the history of Korean literature – what one commentator has called an 'explosion of poetry'. The seven-volume epic *Mount Baekdu*, the first volumes of *Maninbo*, a five-volume autobiography, and countless books of poems, essays, and novels came pouring out. 'He writes poetry as he breathes,' a reviewer once said. 'Perhaps he breathes his poems before putting them to paper. I can imagine that his poems spring forth from his enchanted breath rather than from his pen.' Korean literary critics often call him 'the Ko Uns' instead of Ko Un, because of his incredible activity. A true volcano of productivity, Ko Un has mastered an immense diversity of poetic forms, from epigrams to long discursive poems, epics, pastorals, and even a genre he himself invented, 'popular-historical poetry', of which *Maninbo* is the prime example.

He was invited to spend time as a visiting research scholar at the Yenching Institute of Harvard University, at UC Berkeley, and also, more recently, at Ca' Foscari University of Venice, Italy. He is a Chair-Professor at Dankook University, Seoul. He is also currently President of the Compilation Committee of the Grand Inter-Korean Dictionary.

Ko Un has received a score of prestigious literary awards and honours at home and abroad, including the Björnson Order for Literature (Norway), the Griffin Lifetime Recognition Award (Canada), and the 2014 Golden Wreath Award of the Struga Poetry Evenings (Macedonia).

Some 50 volumes of his work have been translated and published in more than 25 foreign languages, Asian and Western.

VOLUME 11

Hiding the Name

On first meeting,
when a person should introduce himself by name,
he just mutters,
bowing his head.

When he leaves condolence money at a house in mourning
he never writes his name on the envelope,
so when the chief mourner meets him a few months later,
he hesitates to thank him, not sure
whether he paid a visit
or not.

Perhaps he hides his name out of humility,
preferring to have no nameplate or house number in this world
where people love to make their names known.
Or maybe that's not the reason, either.

On general election days
all he does is put a mark on a paper and leave.
When it happens to be a fine day
and flocks of sparrows fly high,
does each individual bird have a name?

Why, a name is a person's prison.

The Entrance to Camp Reagan

After the Armistice,
the village at the gates of Camp Reagan
in Pocheon, Gyeonggi province,
flourished as a brothel town for soldiers.
The instant the camp was abandoned
the town fell to ruin.

The leader of the town's prostitutes
was Rita Kim,
born Kim Ok-suk.

After servicing some hundreds of white soldiers
and some hundreds of black soldiers,
she became the head of the prostitutes' union,
spokesperson and leader
for the whores of Pocheon county.
Her walls were covered with certificates of appreciation
and letters of thanks from local county heads:
'For your contribution to the modernisation of our land...'

Once the Americans cleared out, Korean soldiers moved in.
With the whores gone too,
all that remained of the town were a few small shops.
Kim Ok-suk, left alone, quickly aged and fell sick.
She even stopped swearing as she used to,
'Men are nothing but dicks.'

The High and Low Tides in the West Sea

During the mid-Joseon period,
Korea's submission to China was abject.
In fact the Ming dynasty was on the wane,
but among Korean nobility
submission became all the more prevalent.
For example, faced with the question why
only Korea's West Coast has high and low tides,
and not the East, they replied:

'It's because
China is the source of tides.
Since the West Sea is close to China
it experiences high and low tides,
whereas the East Sea is far away from China,
so no tides can reach there.'

The moment that was said,
the moon emerged from behind a cloud.
They were like dogs barking in that moonlit night.

Hong's Wife in a Shack by Cheonggye Stream

She was probably just the right wife for a man like that.
Just right for her husband the wild boar
who did manual labour,
hurt his back
and was laid up in his room.

She was glib-tongued, that woman.

They had two sons
and three daughters,
kids who never took
to anything like school.

Instead, boys and girls alike,
they took to trouble, taking upon themselves
each and every accident,
from the slums all the way up to
the Willow Tree House at the end of Euljiro.

Early on, the oldest boy did time
in the juvenile wing of Seodaemun detention centre.
Beginning with him,
whenever a son or daughter came home after brawling,
Hong's wife would say,
'Back home? What for?
You should be rotting in the cemetery
in Manguri or Miari.
Scum of a prick's prick,
why haven't you croaked already?
Ayyy! You good-for-nothing, hundred-ton dead weight!'

And yet, though she was a really foul-mouthed woman,
once, when she saw a voluptuous waning moon,
on her way back late at night from the communal loo,
she exclaimed: 'My my my, just look at that goddamn moon!
Looks like the sweetheart I've spent ten million years longing for.'

A Quack

Baek Un-hak rented a room in an inn in Wonjeong-dong, Jeju City
as a master of the *Book of Changes*,
of the *Four Pillars* and the *Eight Characters*.
Meanwhile, another Baek Un-hak was telling tall tales
as a fortuneteller in Jongno 4-ga, Seoul.
In fact, that Baek Un-hak took his name
from the famous fortune-teller Baek Un-hak of late Joseon.

Anyway, whatever the reason,
this other poor Baek Un-hak
(the one who'd crossed over to Jeju Island)
wore plain glass spectacles on his plain nose –
perhaps because his eyes alone had no authority –
and let a few hairs grow out in semblance of a beard.

Maybe in order to impress those who came to consult him,
he would add some ridiculous English
to the fortunes he told.
He also claimed that a true interpretation of the *Four Pillars*
could be found in the philosophy of *fortunà*
as taken back to Italy by Marco Polo.

He pretended to be very intelligent,
very learned.

When he got paid for thus cheating the islanders
day after day, he would go out drinking alone.
Back home, late at night, alone and very drunk,

he would wail and pound on the floor:
Why is it my fortune
that I must ever deceive people?

Such a person, so honest with himself,
might he not be mistaken for the ancient sage Kasyapa
or the apostle Peter?

Third Daughter Seong-suk

Seong-suk's mother
gave birth to her third daughter
as plums outside Jaha Gate were ripening.
On that day, as the plums were falling,
Seong-suk's mother burst into tears
once she realised it was yet another daughter.
She cried, cried loudly, finding no reward in childbirth,
and feeling no hunger after.

So she had no idea at all
whether Seong-suk was born by night
or by day
or at what hour.

Not only Seong-suk's mother,
but her father,
her grandmother, too, had no idea.

Seong-suk grew up
without a name,
her birth unregistered
and her mother always grumbling:
'Begone with you, quickly,
go!'

Her father,
recalling Yi Seong-suk, a girl in Uijeongbu
who once showed him the way,
gave her that name.

Unsure of the day of her birth,
let alone the hour,
she grew up
a very pretty girl,
became a really beautiful young woman,
of such loveliness as is rarely found
even in distant lands –
Portugal, say,
or Sweden.

The Widow in the Central Market

She's known as the Generalissima of the dried fish booths
in Seongdong-gu's Central Market.
If the woman in the next booth over
plays the coquette with a customer,
she cries out, 'Bloody bitch, gone mad again.
She's mad to do what she does by night
again in broad daylight.'

When the Generalissima shrieks,
all shut their mouths, *Shhhh!*
in the dried fish booths,
in the fruit stalls beyond,
in the fresh fish shops,
no matter who's in the wrong.

It's like driest dust being driven from furrows by a strong wind.

Covered by thick awnings,
no sunshine enters the market all day long.

She seizes every opportunity
to squeal like a sow having its throat cut,
cursing her dead husband:
'That goddamn heel, croaked first,
making all this trouble for me, the bastard.'

When it rains, water pools on the awning
then cascades down over her:
'That goddamn Heaven,
goddamn God!'
When people buy dried fish from the Generalissima
for their family memorial rites,
their ancestors' appetites are aroused.

Since the 1970s, cocks seem to crow any time they want,
so the spirits of ancestors can't make out
when exactly it's time to leave;
it's only right, then, that their descendants
should at least arouse their appetites.

Gongju Dawdler

'I hate that song most, "The dawn bell has rung…"
the Saemaeul Song,* I hate that most.'
There was a time you had to be ready to be arrested
if you said something like that.
Even speaking such words took too long.
Such is the dawdling dialect of Chungcheong province.

It's not just in speaking.
Rising
from sitting
takes a long, long time, too.

When they go to Seoul from Daejeon station
they are sure to take the slow train,
which stops at every station,
at every station.
'What would I take
a fast train for?'

When they cross the street,
they slowly start to cross
after coughing three or four times
long after all the other people have crossed.

If a companion urges them on:
'What do you hurry for
so much?
If you hurry, even the rice isn't properly cooked.

'Look at the moon
at night.
It moves
slowly,
slowly,
as if not moving at all.

'If we live by minutes and seconds, we're done for.
It's the same with living by hours.

'Therefore we must have
a night
like half a day, like
early evening,
night,
and early dawn
when the cockerel comes late to the first flap of its wings.
What are you thinking?'

* Song of the New Village (Saemaeul) Movement during the Park Jung-hee era.

The Man in Tapgol Park

Tapgol Park,
a place crowded with elderly folk,
where old men
covered in age spots
grab one another by the collar and sort of fight,
ah!... there he is.

Mansu Coffee Shop
on a side-street in Cheongjin-dong, Seoul,
a place crowded with elderly folk
...there he is.

A place where the elderly roll walnuts in their palms,
sinews squirming on the backs of their hands,
a place where they talk about everything,
shouting this
and that,
and pinch the buttocks of the girl serving coffee,
...there he is.

He's a young man of thirty,
but when asked why he comes here
he says it's the only place he feels comfortable;
when asked his age,
he says he's sixty-five.

They say he was forced to do military service
after he lied about his age,
and his mind was affected
after a beating by a superior in the barracks,
so he was discharged on medical grounds,
and mentally he is old and mad.

Could be so:
the Tang genius, the poet Li Ho, wrote that
at twenty a man is already old.

Father and Son

The father, Shin Gil-ho was 51,
the son, Shin Haeng-bok, 26.
The father had six convictions for larceny,
the son had four convictions for larceny.

In prison, a convict who is penniless is known as *dog hair*,
while one who cashes promissory notes
or cheques is called *tiger hair*.

Dog-hair father and son
were assigned to different cells,
but after supper,
with difficulty, they communicated
through a little barred window in the back.

From the father's third theft
the son
had followed in his father's footsteps.

What they said:
Did you eat enough?
Yes, Dad.
Rub the palms of your hands and the soles of your feet a lot.
And don't skip rubdowns with a cold towel.
Yes, all right, son.

The father, with his shining, prematurely bald head,
murmured to himself:
My boy, I know nothing else about him,
but he's the most filial son in the country.

Jeong Hwa-am

Moving secretly through many parts of China,
he devoted himself to the independence movement in his fatherland.
Along with his devotion and tenacity, he was cautious,
so he survived and came back home.

Even back home, prison was his politics.
His fatherland,
the Korean peninsula
where the sea on three sides can never be calm,
was always the land he dreamed of.

He passed fifty,
sixty,
seventy.

With reality so bleak, even dreaming was hard.

He rejected all honors.
Belief was his only politics.
Even a 40-watt light in a dreary cell
was an utterly vain dream to him
each day when he awoke.

He was no reality, he was a legend.
As if modern history were ancient history,
Jeong Hwa-am endured, white-haired.

The Shit Clan

I have three surnames.
In this land
where changing surnames is one of the greatest humiliations,
I have three or four surnames.

In Japan there is a surname Gui,
meaning ghost,
often therefore changed into the wife's family name.

My case has nothing to do with such customs.
However, my family name can be Kim,
or Nam
or sometimes Jang.

Yet I am no swindler.
Not content with those names, anyway,
I adopt my mother's surname Ko
and am sometimes called Ko.

Once I got dreadfully drunk
and fell into an old-style latrine,
after which I was Bun,
meaning Shit.

Until the 1970s, some eccentrics from the late Joseon period
continued to live with various names like this,
which meant that life was never boring.

My family name was Shit.

The Long-Term Guest at the Dabok Inn in Dadong

Jin Dal-ho
was a man with plans, great or shaky,
who sold his lands in Jeong-eup in North Jeolla
and came up to Seoul.
Though born to the fields,
his body as a whole
was in good shape,
no need for a carpenter to ply his inked cord.

His lips were always fresh,
and when he washed up in the morning
he never gave a damn about others in the queue.
He washed his neck,
behind his ears, beneath his ears,
the ridge of his nose,
even his chest beneath his undervest, two or three times.
He soaped for a long time,
and rinsed off the foam for a long time, too.
Only then did he say: Now I feel alive, I can enjoy my food.
Yet day after day nothing worked out
and he stayed at the Dabok Inn as a long-term guest
for over a year.

His notebook held
the President's phone number,
some National Assemblyman's phone number,
even the switchboard at Midopa department store,
each compactly set down,
but day after day nothing worked out.
All he could manage was
to seduce the woman working at the inn
and make love to her at night.

Three Feet of Rotten Rope

In Yeongdong, North Chungcheong province,
nobody cared about the Yushin Reforms or anything else.
There was one man who took care of all the village's unpleasant jobs
such as renting a room for gamblers,
laying out the body if someone died,
castrating a pig,
mating cows or horses.

That was No Bong-gu.

So poor that the roof of his house rotted into furrows,
but always warm-hearted
like the fire in a brazier.

In the winter when it was too cold to move,
and children walked with short, quick steps,
red-nosed,
he would shelter them from the wind, saying:
'Ah, you must be cold!'

But he was so poor that finally his children were starving.
Somehow he got hold of three yards of rotten straw rope,
tied it to a tree
and hanged himself.
Or rather, pretended to hang himself,
not intending to die.

Once they got wind of that,
the villagers gathered grain
so he and his children could survive
the winter.

'No, it would never do for him to die.
Who would do the hard work
in our village,
in the neighbouring villages,
if not No Bong-gu?'

A Night in Mugyo-dong

The food was seasoned with deep-red pepper powder.
The red pepper that people began to eat
from the late Joseon period
is like something Koreans have eaten since ancient times.
You only have to take a bite,
ahh,
a fire kindles in the mouth.

The drinkers' delight in 1960s and 70s Seoul
was to empty ten bottles of strong *soju*
alongside such hot –
and salty – side-dishes,
when it was already eleven at night, nearly curfew time.

Why did they have to be so tough?

Around that time everything used to get exaggerated.
Even Park Jung-hee got exaggerated,
so that he shrank to bean-size.
If someone shouted
that brat Park Jung-hee,
that brat was even using his daughter as First Lady,
and so on,
that gave him authority
and the friends who had come with him would pay for the drinks.

One day I picked up a scrap of newspaper
off the cement floor of that kind of bar
and first learned about the self-immolation of the young worker
          Jeon Tae-il.

The Time It Takes to Piss

There were plenty of prisoners in Daegu prison with long or life
       terms.
One of the long-term prisoners
with a stiff white beard
looked out into the corridor
and questioned a green youth who had just come from trial.

'What did you get?'
'One year two months.'
'Hell, call that a sentence?
That's the time it takes a lifer to piss.
Hey, how can that be called a sentence?'

Jang Gwang-seop, with his one year two months,
was nicknamed Muhammad Ali.
Even when he got a thrashing from a guard,
he would brush himself off, stand up as if nothing had happened,
and calmly walk away.

This Ali Jang Gwang-seop
was one of the descendants of Jeong Mong-ju,
who stayed loyal to Goryeo to the bitter end
and wrote a last poem before he was killed.
The poem began:
'Though I die
and die again a hundred times...'

An Old Prison Officer

Starting as an errand boy in Gyeongseong jail
long ago during the Japanese colonial period,
he became assistant guard,
then guard,
the lowest rank of prison officer,
for forty-seven years in all.

His work was tying the ropes
and fastening the handcuffs
of those going out for morning sessions,
for interrogations by the prosecution or for trial in court.

His pock-marked face was dark
and his eyes looked as though he had not eaten for three days.
His gold-rimmed hat
sat a little too heavily on him.
When convoy vehicles numbers one and two left early in the morning,
he went along as escort.

In the evenings, as a substitute guard,
he would go peeking into this cell and that,
and if the prisoners kindly offered him
fallen apples or
rice cakes they had bought,
he would take them without hesitation,
with not a word of thanks, saying:
'This rice cake is made with wheat flour,
and coated with soy bean powder.'

For meals he made do with prison food.
When he went home, he did nothing but catch up on his sleep
because he always had triple shift overtime.
That's why he told the prisoners:
'No lifer has anything on me, you know.'

The Person in Charge of Detention Cells at Seodaemun Police Station

In winter it was like the outdoors.
He was the man with hair cut short
in charge of detention cells at Seodaemun police station in the 1970s.
He never got promoted.

Every time someone came in,
every time several came in,
surely they had some fault,
and he would find it,
would kick, kick hard,
to depress their spirits from the start.
Im Cheol-man.

But after meals
he would turn to the women's cell
and demand a song.

If someone sang a song such as,
'I will build a house like one in a picture,'
a storm of applause would pour
from the men's cell.

Then it would be the turn of the men's cell.
If someone jailed for a first burglary after three larcenies
sang 'Camellia Girl'...
Im Cheol-man would scream:
'You lout,
shame on you, you, a man, acting so pathetic.'

A perpetual guard,
he once said in prayerful tones:
'Just one time
these cells
were completely empty
and I was really very bored.

'Yet my wish
is to be in charge of completely empty cells
with nobody coming in.
Hey, you bastard in cell two,
can't you just listen quietly to what I'm saying?
Bastard.'

VOLUME 12

Colette, No Jeong-hye

Colette,
born in Lyons, France,
joined an active sisterhood.
Her younger sister first worked in Vietnam, now lives in Japan.
Colette came to Seoul decades ago.
Her Korean is fluent,
her stomach's accustomed to Korean food.
Even without cheese,
this is her country.

How holy! How amazing!
to have arrived at such intense unity.

Her Korean name is No Jeong-hye.
Secretly, she contributed much to the Korean human rights movement,
starting with the National Democratic Students' Federation incident,
or even before.
She circulated petitions,
collected donations,
hid people,
even promised to hide me.

Her heart's a wide plain.
She made her nest in a Sillim-dong slum,
lived in great poverty.
She reckoned a bowl of instant noodles was a feast.

She alone is reason enough why there has to be religion.

A Blind Man by Saetgang River

No one noticed
how salty it had become,
that river
in Sorae, Gyeonggi Province.

Seo Pil-seok cannot see
that river.
Blind,
he lost his sight some time ago.

At high tide
when rising waters advance to the top of the bank,
his back aches.
He hurt his back long ago in the war,
wounded on the central front.

At low tide
his belly aches,
a problem from long working in that salt farm
where he ended up after discharge.

Later, he lost his sight.
First he had something like cataracts
and the things he saw grew hazier day by day,
until finally he could see nothing.

He thought he'd go mad in that merciless darkness.

Time seems to have been a serum even for that darkness.
He grew resigned,
life a fluttering tent
even for a sightless body.

Today, too,
high tide and low tide depend on the moon.
Old Seo Pil-seok is more a man of the moon
than a man
of the earth.

Muttering

Opposite the primary school in Hwagok-dong
remains one house from the initial development.
Most of the cement blocks in its garden wall have crumbled,
the iron gates have rusted away.
Yi Jeong-gu, owner of that house,
lost his wife a year ago
and slowly went mad, aphasic.

Time just flows, flows on
as he mutters, mutters,
mutters from dawn when he wakes
till night when he falls asleep.

He mutters when the wind blows.
Mutters when it rains.
Mutters when it sleets.

A burglar broke into that house,
heard the incessant muttering from the bedroom,
threw up his hands and ran away.

It happened that a rumour spread
of a Goryeo celadon vase in that old house.
Who knows, maybe someone had already taken it,
leaving behind just the muttering within.
Creepers have grown so wild in the garden
someone could easily be lost and bound...

Dr Jang Gi-ryeo

'Even now, when it rains
I leave the window open
lest I miss the sound
of footsteps
as you approach in the rain.'

Ever since the 4 January retreat in 1951,
he lived in the South,
husband of a divided couple
in a divided country,
never taking a second wife,
sleeping alone in a simple cot.

He settled in Busan and established a modest hospital.
Nobody was ever sent away;
sick and poor,
all received treatment and his loving touch.

For that, he became the model for the protagonist
of Yi Gwang-su's novel *Love*.

It was to meet Jang Gi-ryeo, that holy figure,
like big brother meeting younger brother,
like younger brother meeting big brother,
that the great Quaker teacher Ham Seok-heon,
using other errands as his excuse,
so often travelled down to Busan from Seoul.

Three-headed Hawk

There was once a hawk that had three heads:
with one it looked forward,
with one it looked behind,
and one it turned
to look up and down.

Soaring high into the sky, way up,
it took aim at all of Joseon's corrupt officials.

That's *him*, and *him*, and
there *he* is.

It dived with sharp eyes glaring,
tore at them with its ferocious beak.
In the name of the people,
it hunted out all the grasping officials
so prevalent in the 400 years of the Joseon Era,
sparing but the two hundred men who were clean-handed.

Wondrous!
When the people's most ardent wishes and rancour
ran to the high heavens,
the three-headed hawk went flying up.

Kim Geun-tae

During the 1970s he never stuck his head above water.
While infiltrating this or that dark, dank factory
here and there in Incheon,
he earned several vocational certificates.

He gladly threw away his diplomas
from Seoul National University's Business College and other such.
In the factories he was a respectable *Homo Faber*.

Face like a white candle,
face like a white goat,
but in his brown eyes
a single unwavering resolve
undeterred through decades
would blaze furtively for an instant
then sink back again out of sight.

Since he'd resolved to spend his life united with the workers,
he was known to very few friends
throughout the 70s.
He never surfaced, devoting the intensity of his youth to this task.
He cared nothing for fame or distinction
or any of that, not then nor later in life.

And to his death, he chose to set aside
that other desperate self who had kept a conscious record
of all the tortures he had undergone.

Jei Jeong-gu

After the Democratic Youth Association incident
he did not turn toward groups of intellectuals.
He turned to the poor
and took as wife
one of his comrades
who lived among them.

His face was invisible among the dissidents of the 70s.
His address was a slum,
unlit,
in the darkness after the moon has set.

With that dignity and manly seriousness
a mother admires in a son-in-law,
the more he tried to be modest,
the more he was like a kimchi jar buried in the ground.

'Try to live with contradictions.'
If you lived in the face of such contradictions, you would know:
it's hard just being one of the common folk.

Yun Han-bong

He was fastidious through and through.
He was extreme to a fault.
That is why, even in prison,
after carefully folding up his bedding
he would wipe the cell floor
with a rag, several times.

What purity the word 'enemy' had
when it sprang to his lips
with no hint of eloquence.

He was fastidious even with his comrades.

He remained fastidious
when later he disappeared
in the midst of the Gwangju massacre.
and crossed the Pacific hidden in the bottom of a boat
in the darkness,
in the darkness,
and became Political Exile Number One.

Seo Gyeong-seok

His wife, Shin Hye-su, did not want him to become a pastor.
His mother wanted her son to be a pastor.
He himself so far had no thought of becoming a pastor.
He was simply the son of an admiral,
a graduate in engineering.

He was sentenced to twenty years imprisonment
for the Democratic Youth Association incident,
but he refused to appeal and became a convict.
That was his starting-point.

He hurled himself into the YH sit-in incident in 1979
that paved the way for the collapse of President Park's Yushin
        regime.

Few could compete with him as an organiser.
Wherever he went
he found something to do
which never failed
to lead to yet greater things.

He had a tragic tenacity,
like the sticky sap emerging from the stump
after a large tree is felled.
A tragic tenacity...
even in his glad smile on meeting you after a long absence.

YH's Kim Gyeong-suk

In 1970, the young labourer Jeon Tae-il died.
In 1979, the working girl Kim Gyeong-suk of YH Trading
        plunged to her death
from a rally on the 4th floor of the New Democratic Party
        building in Mapo.

By dying, one opened an age;
by dying, one closed the age.

Behind the grave of Kim Gyeong-suk stands the grave of Park
        Chung-hee.
Go and see.

VOLUME 13

Police Inspector Im Byeong-Hyu

From the information service at Yeongdeungpo police station
he was transferred to Gangseo police station as soon as it opened,
to the No. 2 intelligence section there,
and throughout the Seventies
his job was to accompany one poet everywhere.

The pomade he used
to slick down
his thick hair
smelt disgusting at first
but his companion got used to it.

Whenever that poet went to preside at a wedding
he went along too.
When the poet went to a bar
he'd sit over on the far side
with a glass.
Then,
if the poet went to the bathhouse
after a night's drinking,
he'd go along too,
get into the hot tub naked with him,
and learned to switch between hot and cold tubs.
When the poet went to lecture in Busan, Gwangju, Daegu,
he went along.
When orders came from above,
he'd deploy a combat police unit to keep the poet from leaving home.
A bright-eyed, trustworthy man,
he often wore a blue shirt.
He was reliable but had problems with his wife,
who had no luck with horoscopes and was always quarrelling.
Then, when that poet went to prison,
he deposited the poet's meagre royalties in the bank.

First Love

The full moon rose
over a hillside slum in Bongcheon-dong, southern Seoul.
A young man was climbing the steep path
around 11.30 p.m.
after working overtime.
His name was Yun Sang-gon, he had grown up well,
though knowing nothing of father or mother.

At the top of the steep path
someone was waiting for him in an alleyway, freezing cold.
Her name was Kim Sun-ja.

The full moon was high in the sky.
In a world abounding with the sound of moonlight,
how could poverty be all there was?

Twenty-year-old Sang-gon's tough hand
seized seventeen-year-old Sun-ja's coarsened hand.
Sun-ja had no smell of face-powder.

There was nothing like, 'I love you'.
The young man trembled as he spoke:
'Let's not change.'
Choking, the girl nodded.
She bit her lips in confusion and blood gathered in her mouth.

Won Byeong-o's DMZ

The 38th parallel cut the Korean peninsula in two
from the summer of 1945.
Once again
after the summer of 1950
the DMZ divided the Korean peninsula
with guns aimed across at each other since 1953.

One hundred and sixty miles of barbed wire.
Father in the North,
and son in the South were both experts on birds.

The son in the south tied his name
to a bird's leg and set it loose.
A few years later
the father in the north
set loose a bird carrying his name.

No message.
Had there been a message
it would have been a crime against national security
under the South's anti-communist laws,
and a crime under the North's criminal laws.

Each merely attached his name to a bird,
set it free,
sent it back.
That southern son was Won Byeong-o, a professor at Kyunghee
        University.
The father was an ornithologist in North Korea.

The beauty of blood ties in this time of division
was also the sorrow of the son's
already bald head.

A Fake Blind Beggar

On a corner of Hyoje-dong opposite Jongno 5ga in Seoul
all day long
a blind beggar lay hunched over
wearing dark glasses.

He was murmuring something,
no telling what,
murmuring, murmuring.

Placing before him a ragged cap
he collected 10 *won* coins, 100 *won* coins.
Considering the patient hard work of not moving all day long,
the beggar's wage was far too low.

Apart from occasional crackdowns,
our country offers the freedom and right to be a beggar.

But this beggar, once night fell,
rose to his feet, holding a slender cane,
and quietly headed for the alley of bars
on the slopes of Ehwa-dong.
There he removed his dark glasses and opened blind eyes.

He ordered a drink at his regular bar,
'Hey, give me *soju* and that.'
'That' usually meant a side-dish of spicy fried brawn.

Five years later, that fake blind beggar moved
to the station square down in Jochiwon, South Chungcheong
          province.

A little thief is better
than a thief,
than a big thief.
A beggar is better
than a little thief.
Why, wasn't Sakymuni a chief of beggars?

The Seven-year-old King

In Goguryeo, the nation founded by Go Ju-mong at age fifteen
the royal palace was a thatched cottage.
The waters of the Yalu rose far off.
Day by day the nation prospered.
The cottage turned into an imposing palace.

The sixth king, Taejo,
ascended the throne aged seven.
The king played with his top.
His mother looked after the child-king.

King Jinheung of Silla, too,
became king at seven,
while his aunt exercised royal power.

Isn't regency more than playing the king?

Cheong-dam the Monk

His height when sitting was that of an ordinary person standing
    unnoticed.

While studying at the Jinju Agricultural High School,
and after graduating, too,
he could not for an instant live without Buddhism.
Already married, and one daughter.

First he crossed the sea,
staying at a number of temples in Japan,
then returned to become a monk at Okcheon-sa temple in Goseong,
the Venerable Bak Han-yeong his master.

After studying his fill
he went to deliver a sermon
at Hoguk-sa temple in Jinju, his home.

In the evening following the sermon
his mother came into his room
and produced a kitchen knife from her sleeve.
>   If you don't come back home with me tonight,
>   I'll stab myself in the belly until I'm dead.
>   What I want is a grandson.
He had no choice but to follow his mother
and return to his wife for just that one night.

After that, blaming himself for his apostasy,
he went everywhere barefoot.

And still he nourished great dreams.
So, during the Japanese occupation
he started the National Student Monks' Assembly.
then in 1954 he organised the National Conference of Monks,
establishing the Jogye Order after a sit-in fast
with a hundred monks and a hundred fifty nuns.
He held several posts, such as first General Manager,
Chairman of the Order Committee,
and Supreme Patriarch.

His preaching was not consistent with logic.
He just went on talking endlessly
no way of telling
beginning end
middle
talking all night long until the day shone bright
skipping even the morning chanting.

He died in November of Nineteen Hundred and Seventy-One, at
>   the age of sixty-nine.

Neung-un the Monk

After the Japanese army swept up north in 1592
and the walls of Hanyang, the capital, had fallen,
Neung-un, a monk of Docheon-sa temple, rose up,
gathering seven hundred slow-speaking common folk
in the lower Naepo region of western Chungcheong,

He had always been a stately monk.
Now he tore up his crimson gown, wrapped it round his neck.
With his shaven hair growing long,
his face became that of an angry lion.

He hated the king *and* his officials
for allowing the invasion,
hated them more than he hated the invading Japanese.
His intention was to attack Hanyang
where the Japanese were stationed,
with Yi Mong-hak and others,
and establish a new world.

When Neung-un was executed, heavy rain poured down.

At Evening

On the estuary at Onsuri, Ganghwa Island,
only a couple of boats bobbing,
the hostess of a bar
gazes out
across the mist-shrouded sea.
Her pencilled brows
are lovely.

'It's time they were here...'

She is waiting
for anglers
to arrive on the last boat
crossing from Incheon.
Today she has not had one customer.

On the window of the bar
there is a sheet of yellowing paper:
TURN YOURSELF IN, RETURN TO THE LIGHT.
REPORT ANYONE SUSPICIOUS.

Hyeyung

In the days of the Liberal Party in the 1950s
at Mirae-sa temple in Mireuk Island,
in Tongyeong, South Gyeongsang province,
the disciples of the Great Master Hyobong gathered:
Gusan, Ilgak, Ilcho, Ilgwan and Beopjeong.
Beopcheol and Beopdal were there, too.
And Hwalyeon.

Spring-water-like Hyeyung was also there.
His chanting
sounded like a magpie's squawk.

One day he left abruptly
and without any preparation went up the southern slopes of Jiri
        Mountain.
There, in a small rock cave,
he lived like a wild animal
on roots of trees, wild fruits, other such.

All he had was his koan,
the character Mu (無, Nothingness) of Master Zhaozhou.
Later he would get rid of that, too.

The hair on his head growing long,
his beard growing long, he became a wild animal.

He gave up living as a human being,
and died alone.

It was in the late 1970s
that the animal returned to a human state,
when his bones were reverently gathered up.
They should have been left where they were.
Shameful!

Ho In-su

Maybe it's near that perilous sea at Indangsu
where filial Sim Cheong was sacrificed to the Dragon King
after she sold herself for three hundred sacks of rice
in hope of restoring sight to her blind father –
Baengnyeong Island in the West Sea!
It stretches deep under the sea,
with Jangsangot in North Korea nearby.

There lies freedom for seagulls.
There the young priest Ho In-su spends his days.

He has a bed of lovely little cockscombs in his heart.
He quarrels with no one,
never quarrelled with anyone even in childhood.
When one lyric poem emerges
his joy is such that the time for Mass is a bit delayed.
In Incheon across the sea,
a heated sit-in strike is in progress
at the Catholic Centre in Dap-dong,
but here among the sea breezes of Baengnyeong Island
Ho's clothes are flapping wildly.

Three Family Names

King Hyoseong of Silla had a daughter, the princess Yu-hwang.
The king chose Won Il-sin,
renowned for his filial piety, as son-in-law.
The couple had four sons –
Sam-seok, Sam-myeong, Sam-jae, Deuk-yun.

The two sons Sam-seok and Sam-myeong took their father's
          family name,
Sam-jae adopted his mother's Yu as his surname,
and Deuk-yun, his mother's Hwang.

Later, not those with the family name Won,
but the Yu of Changwon
and the Hwang of Changwon begot descendants.
They were originally a single bloodline,
then diverged into three streams,
flowing on,
flowing on

At times they were indifferent to one another,
like dogs and hens,
at times they desired one another, as hawks hunger for magpies,
and at times they were like a cluster of boils
all breaking out together.

Traveller reaching a village of barking dogs,
a village clouded with evening smoke –
from which family do you trace your descent?

The Cleaner at Okcheon Station

The seats in the slow trains to Busan are hard.
While the trains stop for a while
at Okcheon station
we see a bent-backed old cleaner.

The station is clean,
marigolds bloom in tidy rows,
and cockscombs too.

He pays no heed
to the passing trains,
just keeps on sweeping over and over.

At home, there's no photo of his dead wife.
For him, the inside of the station
is more like home.

He staggers for a moment
in the wind from the new *Saemaul* express trains.

Seol Dae-ui

His American name was David John Seel.
Quite a guy,
quite a guy.

Sometimes a transplanted tree casts a vast shadow.

Arriving in Korea
he spent ten years,
twenty years,
thirty-six years in all.

When he was head of the Jesus Hospital
at the foot of Mount Daga in Jeonju,
once, when a TB patient coughed up black blood and collapsed,
he saved his life by mouth-to-mouth resuscitation.
He sucked in that black blood,
sucked in that dying man's breath.

The first and most sacred task in this world
is saving another's life.

An Unfilial Son is Weeping

Eom Ju-pal, the eldest son of Mr Eom of Hwagokpon-dong,
turned up late for his father's wake.
Late at night,
dead drunk,
he sang an old popular song,
'An Unfilial Son is Weeping'.

Under the awnings people whispered.
His brothers tried to stop him.
Tried,
but they were grabbed by the collars, knocked down
by Eom Ju-pal's powerful fist.

For long ages, men have performed so-called filial and unfilial acts.
Animals are really pure.
Winged animals
and land animals are pure.
Mother and
father
give birth to their young then rear them, and that's all.
They do not live at the expense of their children,
depending on their filial devotion.
Bearing and raising them,
that's the end of it.

What pure disinterestedness.

In general,
exalting filial love quickly leads to exalting loyalty,
and when loyalty is exalted
comes, often enough, dictatorship.

VOLUME 14

Mr Foul-Mouth

On the southern slopes of Namsan
was a spot that just after Liberation
came to be known as Liberation Village.

It was on a steep alley
that twisted so
that once you were inside
there was no way out.
The roofs were head-high.
Mr Foul-Mouth from Pyeongan province in North Korea,
his stiff white hair in a crew cut,
would go up and down,
swearing in a loud voice every day.
'Bloody goddamn...
Bloody goddam...
That f..cking bastard...'

On March 1, 1978, the Independence Movement holiday,
there was no peep from Mr Foul-Mouth,
him with the stiff white hair in a crew cut.

That morning he died, as if to celebrate
the Anniversary of the Independence Movement.

His Own Sword

King Sinmun of later Silla,
came to the throne with the help of Jang Bo-go
who controlled Cheonghaejin, the West Sea.
Therefore
the king's son, when he became the next king,
intended to take the second daughter of Jang, his father's benefactor,
          as his queen.

How could Your Majesty take an islander's daughter as your queen?
Objections came thick and fast.

Hearing of this, Jang Bo-go grew furious
and decided to destroy Seorabeol, the Silla capital:
Outrageous!
Outrageous!

Then the Silla general Yeom Jang
claimed it was he who had complained to the king,
and hastened out to meet Jang Bo-go.

The two of them drank their fill together
and that night, once they were drunk,
Yeom Jang
pulled Jang Bo-go's sword from its sheath
and drove it into his breast.
A great hero who could not be killed by others' swords
had to die by his own.

After that came a time when Korea lost control of the sea,
the sea by which they could cross not only to Okinawa
but to distant Annam.

An Inkstone from Dangye

Chusa Wandang Kim Jeong-hui,
created a new pen-name for himself
every time he produced a piece of calligraphy,
every time he painted.

He ended up having hundreds of pen-names.

His inkstone from Dangye
accompanied him when he was exiled
to Daejeonghyeon on Jeju Island.

It spent its whole life with him,
until at last he wore a hole in it
with so much grinding,
repeated grinding of ink,

and could no longer function as an inkstone.

Its master, Kim Jeong-hui,
got more than a little drunk,
wept,
buried the inkstone
and performed memorial rites before its grave
the following year.

'You left this world ahead of me.'

Countess Yi Ok-gyeong

In the Joseon Era, women had no names.
One girl from the Hong family
was adopted as Emperor Gojong's niece.
Her lips were red as well-ripened boxthorn berries.

The girl grew up
and became the wife of Yi Ji-yong
who was leaving for Japan as Special Envoy;
She accompanied him using the name Gyeong.

She adopted her husband's family name Yi
so she was known as Yi Gyeong.
Her flesh was like white jade,
her teeth like snowy jade
so she was called Yi Ok-gyeong.
Ok means 'jade'.

Once in Japan, on receiving a bribe of ten thousand yen
her husband signed the Korea-Japan Protocol,
then concluded the Offensive-Defensive Alliance for the Russo-
　　　　Japanese War,
allowing the Japanese to use Korea as a military base.

In reality, the whole of Yongsan in Seoul,
some 940 acres,
had served as a base for foreign forces
ever since Japanese forces captured it
during the Imjin invasion of the 1590s.

Finally Korea fell to Japan.
Even a *gisaeng* such as Sanhong refused
to become a concubine of one of the five ministers
who betrayed the nation,
saying that although she was a *gisaeng*
she could never live as the concubine of such a man.

Yi Ok-gyeong, however,
not content with her husband,
had relations with the officials of the Japanese legation:
Hakihara
Kuniwake
Hasegawa.

Her domestic servants used to take her photo
and thrust at the crotch with a stick,
saying, This is a hole for Japs.
A　hole　for　Japs.

Reading the *Maecheon Yarok**
I lingered a moment at this part.

---

* Maecheon was Hwang Hyeon's pen-name, Yarok means 'an unofficial
history'. Hwang Hyeon later committed suicide when Joseon fell to Japan.

Together with Pastor Jeong Jin-dong

A young woman like very fresh young greens,
like young greens
newly washed three times in a flowing stream,
one such young woman,
having dropped out of middle school,
came and sat down in the chilly office
of the Cheongju Urban Industrial Mission.
The room grew even quieter.

Her job was to help a pastor
as bland as long-stored buckwheat jelly
or cold bean curd.

No end in sight once over the edge of the cliff.

Endless days of service.
On her face clean like young greens
appeared a freckle then another and another
like birds singing early in the morning
keeping each other company.

Writing petitions,
writing letters of complaint,
copying out manifestos,
drawing up agreements,

she also had to make visits here and there,
taking long-distance buses over bumpy, dusty roads.
With her face, which never knew make-up,
she devoted all her youth to service
and her laugh was always as it had been
a thousand years before.

No need to know her name.

Kim of Geumho-dong

He has no shoulders.
Shoulderless, he sits
on a rocky ridge in Geumho-dong.

He gazes across the river
at the newly erected apartments in Apgujeong-dong.

Talking nonsense is his job.
Once evening comes,
the lights in the apartments across the river shine bright.

He gazes across at those lights.

He tries to rise,
but his legs have grown stiff, so he has to sit down again
on rocks that have neither blood
nor tears.

An out-of-season mosquito whines
but it has no strength to bite
and he has no blood to suck.
The two of them are in the same state,
Kim of Geumho-dong and the mosquito.

However,
Kim's son
has the best shoulders in Geumho-dong,
a young tough who gives petty thieves a hard time.
Nothing like his father. Nothing.

King Jicheollo

He was first to be given a posthumous name, Jijeung.
He was first to be given the title *Wang* (King)
instead of *Maripgan*.

Jicheollo, the 22nd king of Silla,
had Kim as his family name;
his given name was Jidaero or Jidoro.

This king's prick was said to be well over one foot long.
Unmarried,
he sent agents all over the country
to find him a wife.

At the foot of an old tree in Muryangbu
two dogs
were fighting and biting each other
over a gigantic turd the size of a big drum.

The agents wanted to know whose it was.
They discovered that one village girl
had produced it in the woods
while doing the washing.

As might be expected, that girl was over seven feet high.
She became the wife
of the bachelor king,
a heaven-sent spouse.

The candle was never put out
night after night.
They had two sons
and son Beopheung inherited the throne.

King Beopheung
and his queen both became monks.

Weol-san the Seon Master

A broad-minded fellow
travelling through Manchuria during Japanese rule,
one day he heard the Diamond Sutra being chanted
and became a monk.

Forming an association with other monks,
such as Cheongdam, Seongcheol, Hyanggok,
he sat in the full lotus position
in Bongam-sa temple in Mungyeong,
not lying down to sleep.

With his tall stature he played a major role
in founding the Jogye Order,
then he withdrew into the mountains.

No brilliant poems,
no dazzling sermons.
He simply sat unspeaking, keeping his mind focused,
inside the sound of the wind among Mount Toham's pines,
yesterday,
today,
tomorrow.

Sat upright,
back sheerer than a cliff,
stunning.

King Gyeongmyeong of late Silla

Everything was in decline.
All the lights were going out,
no way things could be put right.
So King Gyeongmyeong in the last stages of Silla
had nothing to do but sit and drink.

Earlier, a dog in a wall painting in the Temple of the Four
            Heavenly Kings barked.
Monks recited sutras
but again it barked.

Then the bow-strings of the five guardians in the temple snapped.
The dog jumped out of the wall painting, barked,
jumped back into the painting.

The seven years of King Gyeongmyeong,
the three years of King Gyeongae
were years of collapse and nothing else.

King Gyeongmyeong asked, Am I a king or a scarecrow?
Drunk,
he took off his heavy crown
and gaped at Mount Namsan in the distance,
which came into sight then disappeared

At night his only care was for one lady of the court, a newcomer.

VOLUME 15

Six Generations of Widows

Among the eighteen sons of King Sejong the Great of the Joseon
       era,
the fifth, Prince Gwangpyeong,
like his father
mastered the Chinese classics by fifteen,
music and mathematics, too,
but died at the age of twenty.
The son he had fathered likewise died young.
Yi Won-hu, the sixth generation descendant of Prince Gwangpyeong,
married at fifteen,
and in addition to his wife,
so also his mother-in-law,
his grandmother-in-law,
great-grandmother-in-law were all widowed young.

Those widows worshipped spirits:
the spirit of the ground outside in the backyard,
the home's guardian spirit inside the house,
Old Granny the kitchen spirit,
the spirit of the outdoor privy,
the Jade Emperor of Heaven and the King of the Underworld in
       the men's quarters.

Spirits everywhere:
The Jade Emperor of Heaven,
The Granny spirit of childbirth,
The Mountain Spirit,
The Farming Spirit,
Wonsa spirits of Wishes,
Joseong Daegam spirits of buildings,
Jeseok spirits of Indra,
Songaksi spirits bringing disaster,
Mimyeong spirits of clothing,
spirits everywhere...

Blind as a Bat

King Sejo of the Joseon era left behind six dead ministers,
and six living ministers.
Kim Si-seup,
one of the living,
became a mendicant monk
wandering the countryside.

Yi Maeng-jeon,
another of the living ministers,
went back home to Seosan, South Chungcheong,
and pretended to be blind,
spending the rest of his life like that,
thirty years,
with a blind man's staff.

Then there was Cheong Rong who pretended to be deaf.
Gwon Jeol too,
after Sejo's bloody coup,
pretended to be deaf.
He even used signs to communicate with his family.

Nam Hyo-on
and his son Nam Chung-seo
pretended to be insane.
If the weather was bad, they laughed: *hee hee hee*.
Even before the weather grew bad they would smack their lips:
        hee hee hee.
When swallows perched on the washing-line,
laughing *hee hee hee*, they sipped wine.

Ten Eyes

The man with ten eyes,
with twelve eyes –

when the moon rises
he looks up at the moon,
at the stars…

He looks up at this star
and that,

even the darkness between the stars.

He can never focus on any one thing,
O Gil-hwan
with his yellowish eyes.

If someone asks:
Hey, Gil-hwan, what did you see last night?
Ummm, I saw everything,
saw everything,
so I don't know what I saw.

A Kkokji Beggar's Values

Gangs of homeless beggars always had a leader, a *kkokji*.
Kkokji had five values to maintain.
Above all,
the gang should not beg from
widows,
widowers,
homes that had lost parents early.
That was called Benevolence.

If a family that has been generous with food loses someone,
the gang should help carry the bier.
That was called Righteousness.

Gangs should not covet each other's territory.
That was called Trust.

If the *kkokji* died
the gang should observe three years of mourning.
That was called Decorum.

The last was called Sense of Shame:
feeling shame at the sun setting in the west
when they stop being beggars and close their eyes.

In the late Joseon period,
the very last, rotten years of Joseon,
it was a poignant task
to rule the world as the beggars did.
So, was putrefying Joseon
destroyed by the Japanese?
Ninety percent of the work was done before they arrived.

Twin Prison Guards

That prison's white wall was so high
that no matter how good you were at flying leaps
or running leaps
or jumping
with a wet blanket
spread wide,

it was absolutely absurd to hope to vault over it.

Twin guards,
Yi Gi-yeol and Yi Gi-sun,

Gi-sun with a birthmark,
spent long years inside that wall
working three shifts,
sometimes only two.

Inside that wall from their 20s through to their late 40s,
surely they were lifers too.

All those years, the older twin, Gi-yeol, beat convicts,
while the younger, Gi-sun,
snatched noodles the convicts had bought.

On each anniversary of their father's early death,
one twin would be on night duty,
the rites attended by his wife and kids alone.
Apart from that anniversary,
Gi-sun stayed in prison most of the time,
but somehow he had three daughters and
two sons, one already lost
in a traffic accident.

Idlers

Outside Yongin town, in Yongin county, Gyeonggi province,
runs a powerful range of mountains
and there, in the valley below the tomb of Jeong Mong-ju,
spring had never a thought of coming.

In Seoul,
and along the banks of the Hantan River above Seoul
the forsythia was already in full bloom

Yongin, however, often known as 'Posthumous Yongin',
was always 'Late Yongin'.
The cold spring winds
had an icy edge.

The loudspeakers of the New Village Movement
pestered the village of Mansuteo
from early morning,
while just two people,
Jin Su-mun and his wife Gang Hye-ja,
exhausted
after making love that morning,
slept on,
shhh
shhh,
stretched out with bare stomachs,
though the sun was high in the sky.

Then Jin Su-Mun was bitten by a centipede.
Damn it!
It bit me in the privates.
Damn it!
Damn it!

Notorious as a couple of idlers,
they had never received a New Village loan,
yet they were carefree and could always be heard shouting,
Damn it!

Walking Sticks

On the grounds of Buseok-sa temple in Yeongju, Sobaek Mountain,
there is a tree that grew
from a walking stick
planted by the great monk Uisang.

In Songgwang-sa temple in Suncheon, South Jeolla,
there is a tree that grew
from a walking stick
planted by the deeply revered monk Bojo, of the Goryeo dynasty.

The trees have lived long lives,
two thousand years,
one thousand years.

Nearer us, there's a maple tree on Jungdae peak of Odae-san
that grew from a stick the Venerable Hanam
rested on
then planted.
It put out leaves and branches,
the leaves turning red in autumn.

One poet during the Yushin period in the 1970s,
sat beneath such walking stick trees
on Odae-san's Jungdae
and in Jogye Mountain's Songgwang-sa temple
while confined there by the intelligence agency.

Before him sat the elderly police detective, his keeper,
who said: 'Well, thanks to you
I'm enjoying life as a mountain hermit,
the cicadas singing by day,
the Scops owl by night.'

Replied the poet:
'Hey, since you walk about
with a stick,
you should plant it when you leave.
Who knows?'

The Yu Brothers, Grave Robbers

The world is so full of robbers
that there is no rest
even for graves.

Come to think of it,
surely a poet is a robber of birdsong,
robber of the sound of streams,
of the colour of flowers, of willow leaves.

A robber who dug up graves
was known in days past as a 'grave-digging thief',
writ using difficult Chinese characters
by those sporting a nobleman's hat and gown.

The graves of rich families' ancestors
were laid out ceremoniously, following ancient rules,
so when they were dug up,
those graves of great-great-grand parents,
of great-grandparents,
of grandfather,
of grandmother –
even if they held no treasures –

when told that a skull or bones had been dug up,
the family had to produce a wad of money,
as much as the robbers asked,
to get back the sacred remains.

Those descended from the nobility, from the *yangban* class,
understood well how *yangban* worshipped their ancestors.
They were themselves the robbers
of the grave sites.
The robber brothers, Yu Seung-ok and Yu Guk-hyeon,
were direct descendants from *yangban*
who had been expert at digging up graves.

By day they had looked most fine,
their way of clearing their throats had great dignity.
When a ripe watermelon is cut open
it is red and dignified.
The French robbers who in times past
dug up the grave of Prince Namyeon,
they must have looked fine too.

A Police Spy

The Writers' Council for the Practice of Freedom
had no office,
so if the chairman was walking along a street,
that street was the office,
the bar where the secretary was sitting was the office.

It was the second dissident group
that the Park Jung-hee government decided to eliminate.

When they got together in a bar
outwardly it might have looked as if they were enjoying a drink,
but secretly
they were discussing a rally or a declaration on the situation
they planned to issue a few days later.

Eom Ok-nam
was sure to appear at every such gathering,
saying he admired writers with such upright minds.
At times he would pay for a third round of drinks,
contribute some *bulgogi*,
even buy the chairman a new suit.

That tall Eom Ok-nam with large whites to his eyes
was a police agent who reported every detail
to the CIA headquarters on Mount Namsan.
He only pretended to be a fan of the writers.

Later it was learned
he was separated from his wife,
had been kicked out
after extorting money from his wife's family.

When he went to the bath house
he would come out four hours later,
saying:
'Ah, I feel better now.'

Little Ham Seok-heon's Teacher

When Ham Seok-heon was a child
at a village school in Yongdangpo, North Pyeongan province,
the teacher of the calligraphy class
took great care of the students,
stooping over them
as they wrote one character after another.

His students also had to learn
to grind the ink steadily
and hold the brush firmly.

He would snatch the brush from an awkward student's hand.
Grabbing the boy's hand from behind, he would say:

'You little brat,
how will you make your writing strong
if you hold your brush as weakly as that?

'Japanese writing may be pretty,
but our writing must above all be strong.'

Jeong Jeom's Grandmother

Something like a mass of red-bean gruel
hangs dangling,
off almost the whole left side of her face.
It looks as if gruel boiled up
for some time
before stopping where it did.
Seen one way, it is gruel,
another, a human face.

Luckily or unluckily,
the eye and eyebrow on the right side are attractive.

Notwithstanding,
during her lifetime
she had a husband,
gave birth to sons and daughters,
and now her grandchildren run away from her.

Jeong Jeom's grandmother with her red-bean gruel
wears double-decker gold rings,
two, in case one might seem insufficient,
on her quite swollen finger.

Not only her face: her finger too is weighed down.

Two Singers

They never made a hit.
But though they would never be famous
they were people who just loved singing,
regardless of the season, spring or autumn

Among those singers,
was a sensible girl.
who lived near the bank of Wansan stream on Omokdae Hill in
        Jeonju.

Having heard of her
somehow or other,
a middle-aged singer came to visit
from Geumgu in Gimje at the foot of Moak Mountain

His traditional jade-green coat and white rubber slippers were
        gorgeous.

Bowing politely, he said:
'I have come to hear your unusual voice.'
The young girl greeted him just as politely.

Then the girl and the man
spread a rush mat on Omokdae Hill,
brought out drum and fan,
tested the drum. They worried
the drum's leather had grown slack because of the weather
or its strength been sapped for lack of use.

'I have neither natural talent nor good discipline,'
said the man,
'so please listen with a generous heart.
First I will sing a *danga*
inviting you to sing.'

The man sang a *danga*:
'Flowers are blooming on this hill and that...'
Once his sometimes sonorous,
sometimes delicate singing ended,
he bowed politely
and took back the drumstick.

Now the girl rose softly to her feet,
lifted her scarlet skirts slightly,
opened the fan,
began the first passage from the *Song of Chunhyang*.

Her dazzling voice,
flowing over and pouring out,
joined with the stream below.

The man rose, saying:
'I have heard most precious singing.'
The girl stood there, replying:
'Oh no, not at all.
I am humbled and grateful that you have listened.
May you have a safe journey home.'

An Elderly Comfort Woman

A passage in Kakou Senda's
Military Comfort Woman says:
An old Korean woman of sixty
living in Japan
was never able to return to her own country.
In the colonial period
she was a sex slave for Japanese soldiers.
Some days she serviced 300 or 320.

Don't be surprised.
If each man took a minimum of three minutes,
that means she lay there for seventeen hours with legs spread.
In spite of that, she did not die.

This happened in the South Pacific, in remote Rabaul.
It might have been better
had she been bitten by a cobra and died.

Because of the soldiers' inflamed desire,
having never seen a woman for months and months,
the women never had a day off.

That comfort woman,
that old Korean Japanese woman
died beside a small brazier in an old tatami room.
Skin covered her bones,
clothes covered her skin,
so she was no longer a comfort woman.

I will not mention her name here.

A Child

One very cold day in January, 1978, thirteen or fourteen below zero,
there were some 130,000 shacks on the outskirts of Seoul,
housing one and a half million people
who leased with key money deposits,
or rented some of the smallest, just 5 *pyeong* in size
or 12.

All told, one-fifth of Seoul's seven and a half million
lived in shacks
on the banks of streams,
on hillsides,
on scraps of suburban land.

Shacks covered with planks and roofing,
in Sadang-dong,
Bongcheon-dong,
Sillim-dong,
Siheung-dong,
Changsin-dong,
on the banks of Cheonggye Stream, Jungnang Stream.

One latrine for twenty households:
fierce fights at the latrines from early morning on.

An abandoned child
in a steep alley between the shacks
in Sadang 4-dong
was fourteen years old
but looked thirty.

What's your name?
Ju Man-seok.
The naked child stood with his penis bluish in the cold,
his drooping penis looked forty.

And yet,
and yet,
a smile remained,
a flower-like smile,
or rather,
that of a child with chronic intestinal problems,
a dried-up smile.

A Day without Beggars

When John Foster Dulles came a-visiting
in the time when the Liberal Party ruled,
and after that
when Henry Kissinger came,
and in 1979 when Jimmy Carter came,
the Korean Ministry of Home Affairs
rounded up every last beggar
on the streets of Seoul
and locked them up in a camp in Nokbeon-dong.

No beggars here.

Beggars with only one leg,
beggars with only one arm,
beggars pretending to be deaf and dumb,
beggars so sick
there was no telling when they would die,

and beggars unable to get fifty won in a day,
or the opposite,
beggars who threateningly thrust out a wide open hand
glaring as fiercely
as did wounded veterans in the streets in the 50s,
all such beggars were swept away.

No beggars here.

Human nature comes in two varieties,
that of a thief or that of a beggar.
A day without beggars is a day for thieves.

Carter,
I hope you and your mysterious, beguiling smile
scamper back to Washington quickly.

VOLUME 16

Seung-ryeol's Tomb

If the Soviet guards catch you, you're done!
That evening
it was raining steadily.
A few families, escaping southward,
inched across the mountains, holding their breath.

At last they reached the 38th parallel.

If the Soviet guards catch them, they're done for!

As they crossed the line
a baby started to cry.
Its mother muffled the sound
swaddling the baby in a blanket.

Finally they were safe.
The guide, once paid, vanished.
On the sodden ridge, scratched by the brushwood,
they all sighed with relief in the rain.
We're alive, they gasped.
We've made it,.

The blanket muffling the baby was unwound.
The one-year-old
was dead, suffocated.
The mother shook her dead baby.
She shook it
and wailed.

'Seung-ryeol, Seung-ryeol, Seung-ryeol... Seung-ryeol.'

The father, having no spade, dug a hole in the earth with his bare hands.
He snatched the baby's body from her arms and buried it.

Seung-ryeol,
Seung-ryeol,
Seung-ryeol...

Elena

She was born in early spring 1940
near a fresh green barley-field, skylarks soaring.
Her mother lacked milk so went round the village with her infant,
and she survived thanks to the milk other mothers gave grudgingly.
So her life began as a baby beggar.
From the age of six
she started doing night work, keeping her mother company.
So she set out on a wearisome life as a child labourer.

After the war
she was sixteen, quite beautiful.
When she smiled the slightest smile
dimples appeared on both her cheeks.
Desolate times though they were,
some bright angel seemed to have alit upon her eyes.

In the summer of 1956
on her way home from evening classes
she was raped
by two US soldiers in a jeep.
She wanted to die.
She wanted to die.
Even heaven no longer existed.

And her hometown was no refuge;
it was a place of pointing fingers.

Weeping
she left home and,
as fate would have it,
became a whore outside a US base in Songtan, Geonggi province.
Sunja turned
into Elena.

In a drunken fit she killed a US private
who was hitting her, refusing to pay.

Sentenced to life,
Elena
turned back into Sunja.
She was sent to Suwon prison,
then to Gongju prison,
then to Suncheon prison.

Never once did her lips speak the word 'love'.
When everyone around the world was talking
about Eisenhower being elected president,
she remained silent for a whole day.

Mute. And in her heart, a clot of ash.

Others' Eyes

That war
took away the greetings we used to exchange even with strangers.
It took away customs of speaking slowly,
gently.
Words became faster
and sharp.
That war took away the clarity in the eyes
of people in autumn's cool wind.
Gradually,
not only the eyes of people
but of cows and horses in the stony fields
grew bloodshot and fierce.

In front of Daejeon Station
a gum-selling kid
was clearly beating another kid to death.
Not one spectator
intervened. The wind stirred up the dust.

Not one
had the friendly face of villagers back home.

Two Rivers

Of a sudden
shortly before the Armistice
the fierce fighting on the western front
stopped.
No sound of gunfire,
anywhere.
Was that an illusion?

Once again the sound of gunfire
filled the space between enemies.
Rain began to pour down.
Illusion?

That night
Byeon Ju-seop, a youth from Pyeongsan, Hwanghae province,
crossed the Yeseong River in the rain.
Bare-footed,
he kept on, heading over mountain ridges.
Finally, more than exhausted, he crossed the Imjin River
oblivious of the pain of his bleeding feet, their cracked soles.

When the boy reached the southern bank of the Imjin River,
his constant dream for several days,
he called out repeatedly, Mother! Mother!
his whole body shivering,
upper and lower jaws
trembling each on their own.

The rain kept on.

Mother was in the North now, son in the South.

His voice changed.
His face was full of freckles.

Now he was alone.

He would be alone when he begged,
when he filched.
He would be alone when he delivered restaurant food.
Alone, oblivious of a future in which he would father eleven children.

He had a triangular face.
He cried wildly, calling, Mother! Mother!
The division of North from South
divided one from one, one from another, individuals.
After that day the youth no longer wept.

His brows were bushy.
He did not weep even when, much later,
in a printing shop, his finger was severed by the cutter.

Old Sim Yu-seop

War widows need their smokes.
When you miss someone, you have to have a smoke.
When the person you miss has disappeared,
you have to have a smoke.
Widows, and widowers must develop a taste
for tobacco.
Friends separated forever from friends
must develop a taste for tobacco.

One nation was divided into two.
The moment of division,
the two became enemies.
Naturally,
inevitably,
absurdly,
war broke out.

For a few months the front line moved ever farther south.
It engulfed even the west of South Gyeongsang province.

The American fighter planes changed abruptly:
one moment, Second World War propeller-driven Grumman
          Hellcats;
the next, jet-propelled Sabers.

Then the front line shot up northward.
More and more North Korean troops retreated.
At first, the North's advance had been unhindered,
now the advance by the South was unhindered.

The whole country was turned into scorched earth
from carpet bombing by the US Air Force.
Who among us had wanted scorched earth?
Was it ruins
we so ardently desired?

While the fighting moved up
and down,
the rice was ripening
in the fields round Jochiwon, South Chungcheong province.

Sixty-five year-old Sim Yu-Seop,
having given his paddy fields a triple summer weeding,
was waiting wordlessly
for the autumn harvest

His heart was entirely given over to his two sons.

While the country changed names,
from the Republic of Korea
to the People's Republic,
and then from the People's Republic
back to the Republic of Korea,

his elder son was a soldier for the South,
while the younger had gone off to volunteer for the North.

Even when the dog wagged its tail,
Old Sim's lips wouldn't open.

Soon he'd be marking the third anniversary of his wife's death.
He felt lonely, he whose old nickname was 'thin-as-a-post'.

More than himself,
his shadow was 'thin-as-a-post'.
In all his sixty years
he had only ever told three or four lies.
He, too, needed to chain-smoke:
cigarettes rolled from dried tobacco leaves.

The Lake

I grew up in the Bujeon Highlands, South Hamgyeong province.
If I climbed over the mountain, panting,
I could gaze down at Bujeon Lake.
I wanted to stand there
forever
like the trees, like the dead trees there by the lake.
And I wanted my dead friend Jin-man
to come stand with me for a really long time.

The lake was a place the spirits of the departed visited.

At the time of the January 4 Retreat
when tens of thousands were swarming southward,
I was lucky to manage to embark on an American navy LST,
a 100-to-1 chance, 150-to-1.
Tens of thousands who failed to get away were without hope.
Surrounded by anxiety and fear, I rode all the way down to Busan.

I became a night worker on number 3 dock in Busan,
then a deliveryman for a Chinese restaurant,
a carrier of relief goods at Gukje Market,
a gangster,
a jailbird doing time for violence,
a gangster again.

Once only did pure passion erupt from deep in my heart:
I fell in love with Miss Kim who worked in a tea-room
and gave her a gold ring for her birthday.
After I went to jail
she disappeared somewhere,
Seoul, perhaps,
or Dongducheon.

Throughout those hectic days,
steadfast was my own Bujeon Lake,
which lay behind me,
beckoning me to come,
come back, quickly.

I lost my left arm in a gang fight in Nampo-dong, Busan.
I am called Left-armed Yeong-nam.

Despair

On October 5, 1950, when Seoul was recaptured
after three months' occupation by the North,
hope was everywhere.

By a low shack where the stream's murmuring was always heard
outside of north Jaha Gate, Seoul,
surely the apricot trees would blossom next spring?

The daughter of that house, as she lay in bed sick,
was raped by a man in a UN jacket.

She collapsed,
the man spat, then vanished.

On roadside telegraph poles, flyers were posted:
Long live President Syngman Rhee! Long live General MacArthur!

Hope was everywhere.

Young Jun-ho

After scattering his father's ashes
over the fast-flowing stream
from the dusky bank of the Seomjin River,
the boy looked up
toward Nogodan Ridge.

It was shrouded in cloud.

From now on fourteen-year-old Jun-ho,
wherever he is, will live without a father,
starving one day in three.
The wind will always be against him.

The boy takes after his father, chip off the block.

Commie's kid,
Commie's kid:
that name will stay with him all his life.

Bachelor Kim

Prisoner number 7501.

They called him 'number seven thousand five hundred and one'.
They called him 'seven five o one'.
Sometimes,
they called him
Bachelor Kim.

He came in aged 27 –
forty-five years of solitary confinement in a tiny cell
The day came when he was released, aged 72.

At dawn his cell door opened.
'You've had a hard time,'
his first warm greeting.

A firm conviction that still sometimes blazed up
was lodged firmly inside his withering body,
utterly unchanged.

Bachelor Kim.
He entered as a youthful bachelor,
exited an elderly bachelor.
His clear, high-pitched voice
was rarely heard
under a forehead sunk like a weathered grave.
He was taciturn.

His real name was Kim Seon-myeong.
He was a soldier in the People's Army, then a POW.
Despite the Geneva Convention
he was first sentenced to death,
then to life imprisonment.

As a child, all the land
for miles around was his family's.
He was the son of a man whose land yielded ten thousand bushels,
10,000 bushels, annually.

Afterwards,
the war between South and North
immured one young man in prison for so many years.
He once said to someone that living is better than dying,
– sure, *living*.
Bachelor Kim's remaining life was the life of a stone
sunk in water all on its own.

Man-su's Grandma

They barely avoided the miseries of a refugee camp.
They built a shack at the top of Dodong hill opposite Seoul Station.
The family of five felt blessed.
However, Mansu's grandma had lost her wits
amid the crowds of people fleeing
in the winter of 1950.
'Let's go,
let's go,
let's go home,'
she used to insist after pissing on the floor.

Her son Sun-gon was a porter at the railway station.
Her grandsons Man-su and Man-gil delivered newspapers at dawn.
They ate dark brown soup with dough flakes twice a day,
around a small circular table.

The old woman poured out curses
at her daughter-in-law in the kitchen:
'You bitch, you brought me here,
bitch, you brought me here to kill me,'
and then she sobbed,

and continued to shout:
'Let's go,
let's go,
Sun-kon,
let's go home.
Let's leave that bitch behind and go.'
The nights were all hers.

She had never been more than a mile or so from home.
Born at the foot of Cheonbul Mountain in South Hamgyeong province,
on marrying she moved to the nearest village
over the hill,
lived there for sixty-six years.
Then she was brought hundreds of miles down to unfamiliar Seoul.

'Let's go,
let's go,'
that was all she said,
never removing the towel wrapped round her head.

The House with Wooden Tiles

Sacred, truly sacred, is the smoke rising as evening rice is being
        cooked!
Until August 10, 1945,
Korea was a single whole.
Since August 10, 1945,
Korea has been two.
America it was that proposed dividing the peninsula at the 38th
        parallel,
American forces occupying the South,
Soviet troops the North.

The Japanese surrender
on August 15, 1945
was supposed to signify the liberation of Korea.
In fact, it signified
the division of Korea.

The 38th parallel passed through an old wood-tiled house,
a house built by slash-and-burn farmers
on a hilltop above the Soyang River in Inje County, Gangwon
        province,
at the waist of the peninsula.
Northern guards occupied it.
Southern guards challenged them.
Both shouted: It's our house,
it's our land.
Each threatened the other,
firing blanks.

Then someone had a bright idea:
What about demolishing
the house altogether?
That's it!

The house roofed with wooden tiles in that remote valley,
a house inhabited by four generations,
vanished.
The owner, Im Bong-sul, aged sixty-four,
and his granddaughter Im Gasina, aged fourteen,
left carrying bags and bedding.

The old man wept all the way, without shedding tears.
The little girl did not cry.
She stared down at the Soyang River below,
a river she would never see again.

Homecoming

At the end of June 1950
5th-year middle-school student Kim Myeong-gyu enlisted as a
            volunteer.
His regiment
kept retreating on the pretext of relocating.
While Dabuwon above Waegwan
was captured and recaptured dozens of times,
he survived.
How is it that he survived?
one of just nine survivors in his platoon?
His face was covered with pimples.

After Seoul was recaptured,
he came back home,
carrying his rifle.

His long-widowed mother
and his older brother Se-gyu
had been killed by the withdrawing communists.
The neighbours held a welcoming party for him.

He spent one day
at his mother's grave
and his brother's grave.
He even paid a visit to his father's grave,
whom he had never seen.
Late that night, a shot rang out.
He had killed himself.
A couple of *soju* bottles lay beside him, toppled over.

Yang Hyeong-mo

Snow drove furiously down
onto the eight-year old.
        Where are we?
        Where are we?
Fields in a blizzard.
During the 4 January 1951 retreat,
behind a railway station near Pyeongtaek, Gyeonggi province,
double-cropped barley fields were covered with snow.
Some eighty refugees wrapped in straw sacks
huddled on the ground in snowdrifts.

Among them
were Hyeong-mo, his father and mother,
with his two younger brothers.
How lucky they were to have survived together,
all the family.
How lucky they were, starving together and
eating together.

Toward nightfall, Hyeong-mo left to get firewood.
Boom!
A shell fell, fired in error.
The eighty went flying, vanished.

Hyeong-mo came rushing back.
Father,
mother,
brothers, gone.
Baek Seung-bok's family, too,
who came south with them,
all the way from Jinnam-po, in South Pyeongan province.

Around the pit made by the shell
were a forearm,
a shoe,
a severed head,
a pair of glasses,
a corpse that was groaning then stopped groaning.

After that, Hyeong-mo, wrapped in a tattered blanket,
followed an orphan's path, with no direction,
no north, south, east or west.

The blizzard stopped.
He shouted up at the frozen sky,
calling for mother, for father.
He called for his brothers, too,
Hyeong-jin!
Hyeong-ryeol!

The Old Widower

In winter 1955 the whistles of Seoul-Busan trains could be heard
        faintly
in a remote village in Yeongdong, North Chungcheong province.
If there were train whistles to be heard,
the world was still the same world.
The hills were all bare together,
they would shiver at night.
Bare, the hills all looked the same,
no telling which was which.

Ocheon Mountain,
Mireuk Mountain,
Chotdae Peak,
the hill in front,
the hill behind Ssangbong village,
no telling which was which.

What the children drew were
always
bare, red hills,
hills of red clay.
Even the bellowing of oxen
was a red bellowing.

Over the ridge of one such hill, as the sun was setting,
a person was coming, slow and weary.
Who could it be?
Who other than a man
half insane,
half in his right mind?

Wife
and two children were killed
together by a mortar shell,
one ox was also killed.

He alone survived,
Yi Jong-su, a fellow with thick hair.

He had a high-pitched voice
like a wild goose.

Several millions died in the course of three years of war.
Among the dead
were Yi Jong-su's family.
In the empty stable
all he could say was:
'Hey Wife, hey Wife!'
and then
'Jang-seop!
Cha-seon!
Cha-seop!'

Shin Hyeon-gu

Why do you know of nothing but your home village?

In Onjeong-ri, across from Daegwanbong village,
on the southern slopes of the Myeorak Mountain Range,
in Pyeongsan County, Hwanghae province,
out of forty-seven inhabitants
nine left with the People's Army.
Onjeong-ri was a village with one mule,
five dogs,
and twenty-three rabbits.
Lots of mice, too.
Wild cats and badgers would appear by turns,
and a family of three wild boars used to come down
and trample the potato fields.
Sometimes a stately flock of ravens would alight.

When the mule neighed,
the chimneys that sent the suppertime smoke
soaring, soaring high
would listen to the mule's neighing.
Fifteen-year-old Shin Hyeon-gu kept having mishaps.
He would get scratched bloody by holly leaves,
or hurt his hand while cutting wood.
He hoped one day to become a monk.

For that fifteen-year-old Shin Hyeon-gu,
the village he'd grown up in grew suffocating.
He was like a mule, like a baby wild boar,
that suddenly goes wild.
Luckily the war spared the village.
In his dreams, wings sprouted from his shoulders.

On a bitterly cold night
when ice nine centimetres thick was cracking,
hordes of Chinese volunteers
surged across the Yeseong River
after crossing the Yalu,
the Cheongcheon,
and the Daedong.

On that night Shin Hyeon-Gu
swam across the Yeseong River downstream from the ferry,
carrying two of his mother's rings.
Her ancestor had been one of the leaders of the Donghak Uprising.

Air came through his nostrils, and water, too.
After fifteen minutes,
he reached Saemal on the other bank.
He pulled on the clothes he had rolled up and tied to his body.
They were clothes of ice.

When he turned around he seemed to hear his mother's voice:

'You alone at least
must live.

Off you go.
Off you go.'

Her words remained in his ears.
Mother!
He called out in the direction of the village he had left.

Decades of Armistice passed after he left home like that.
He was 63, had two sons, three daughters, and seven grandchildren.
One daughter was divorced, one not married.
In the darkness at the crack of dawn, those old rings,
at daybreak, those rings alone remaining from the past,
were the only strength left to him.
At heart he was always crossing rivers and going over mountains.

The Refugee Camp in Songtan

It was called a refugee camp
yet had not so much as an iron fence.
It was
simply a place, beyond Sut Pass,
where people put up second-hand tents
or built shacks with pieces of plywood,
to keep out the wind and rain.

We heard that Chinese troops would soon be coming
like a swarm of locusts.
We had to move again, from Songtan
to Jochiwon or to Daejeon.

Could be we might end up in Busan, the provisional capital.
Amidst all this confusion
Yu Byeong-cheol's wife, from Sinanju in the North,
gave birth to a son.

Huddled in ragged quilted clothes, Yu Byeong-cheol
had it seems held on to a scrap of artistry.
He exclaimed with a laugh, 'A migrant bird's been born,'
and rejoiced, drinking a quart or more of cheap *soju*.

Yi Jeong-sun's Spirit

Over at last: the three months of the People's Republic.
Its local committee members
had to run away.
But they did not just run away
with eyes burning.

They took 150 people with them,
saying that they had to do night work at the aerodrome,
pushed them into air-raid shelters built by the Japanese army
near the end of the Japanese occupation.
The 150 were buried alive,
stabbed with bamboo spears
until their hearts leaped out,
stripped naked and raped,
beaten over the head
with stones.
They were pushed inside alive
and covered with earth.

In retribution against her right-wing father,
former head of the irrigation association,
they buried his lovely only daughter, Yi Jeong-sun,
after they had gang-raped her.
Pretty much a rotting corpse,
yet how peaceful
was her dead face, eyes so quietly shut,
how very peaceful.

About a year later,
the war was still far from over,
Yi Jeong-sun appeared in a dream to her friend Go Ok-hui
who lived in Okjeong-gol.

'Ok-hui!
I've come back.
Our dog
used to leave marks of its journey
by pissing
as it followed mother across the fields.
I, too, left marks up there in heaven,
so I could come back now
without getting lost along the way.'

Go Ok-hui woke up and wept, alone. The first cock began to crow.

Widow Mun

Her husband,
her tender-hearted,
slightly pockmarked,
generous-hearted husband,
was early requisitioned by the Japanese
as a labourer in the Pacific islands,
and never came back.

Field work and rice-paddy work, all was hers now.

Their older son grew up.
The younger one was born posthumously. He, too, grew up.

During the Korean War, the elder son joined the army
and never came back.
Nobody knew whether
he was alive or dead.

The younger boy, who had never seen his father,
went downtown
and on his way home,
though still only a lad,
got dragged off by the national defence corps.
It was talked of much later. Those were dark days.

She went out alone to weed the paddy field a second time
at the height of summer heat.
The sun beat down mercilessly
on the back of widow Mun of the Nampyeong family.
As Lao Tzu said:
Heaven is not benevolent.

The Fields That Winter

Winter fields rest well.
If their owner is industrious
they are harrowed
then exposed to the icy wind,
and they rest well.

A notification of death-in-action arrived – a mimeographed form.

The box with the remains of their son,
staff sergeant Kim Seung-ho, did not arrive.

In that single day,
his father, Kim Chil-seong,
aged from fifty-one
to something like seventy.

Leaving his wife wailing and beating the floor.
he went out into the winter fields
alone.

There was nowhere to look. He smoked his third cigarette.

123

One Kitchen

There is nothing but the Duman River
outside the town of Gyeongseong, North Hamgyeong province.
People sowed millet
in stony fields,
and it grew.

Despite the bitter cold
it managed to survive into the following spring.
On the day the one worm-eaten peach tree blossomed
the women smiled brightly.

The poor family of An Deok-su
lived on good terms with Bak Gi-jun's family,
sharing a kitchen.

The two families
would cook together
and share the food.

On days when the two families quarrelled,
An Deok-su's family
would cook first and eat,
after which Bak Gi-jun's family
would prepare their meal and eat.

When An Deok-su's daughter Il-sun
and Bak Gi-jun's son Seong-ho
went into the willow grove on the sandbanks in the Duman River
and didn't come back,
the two families went out to search for them.
They became in-laws.

Poverty divides people,
and it brings them together.
When reclaimed land is continually trodden down
it becomes firm.

Home

About 3,000,000 people moved South;
more than 100,000 moved North.
Those 100,000 were welcomed splendidly.
But one by one they disappeared
until few remained.

The 3,000,000 who came South were like roots.
They kept saying
they were uprooted
but their roots went deep.

A home is a grave on a hill buried in the heart.
A home
is the memory of one who has left it behind.
A home exists in time.

That 10,000,000 families are divided between North and South
is one fact of modern Korea's history.
It is not a past that we should go back to,
but the start of tomorrow.

 I want to go back. I want to go back.
 I want to go back to a home on the banks of the Duman River.
 I want to go back to my home beside the Daedong River.
 I want to ride a sleigh there.
 Mother,
 are you still alive?

There was one,
O Jong-cheol,
who did not linger in the past.

Born in Wonsan, South Hamgyeong Province,
he crossed the 38th Parallel southward shortly after Korea became
   independent.
He lived like a mole.
He lived as a penniless sluggard.

Then, reborn, he studied at an evening college,
set up a textile factory and
a leather goods factory.

He never once talked about home.
He bought a hill, bought vast rice fields
in Yeoju, Gyeonggi province.
He set up empty graves for three generations of his ancestors.
On the autumn harvest memorial day, they were his home village.

Ortega Kim

Time brings today and yesterday together.
Time brings here and there together.
Even long-lasting sorrow
cannot but be the veins of time.

His mother wore a black skirt and white blouse made of cotton.
She never wore any other clothes.
When she came home from the millet field
and removed the towel from her head, she was beautiful.

To the son
who left his mother
in a remote village in Uncheon, North Pyeongan province,
time meant here and there.
That image of his mother in black skirt and white blouse from
        fifty years ago
stuck with him, unchanging.

Kim Yeong-man, a sixteen-year-old in the People's Army,
came down South from the North.
His battalion came down
as far as Yeosu
on the Southern Sea.
They crossed the Seomjin River
to attack Masan.

He soon forgot his familiar landscapes.

He was taken prisoner during the Masan assault.
In the prisoner-of-war camp on Geoje Island
fervent communist prisoners were fearless together.
The anti-communist prisoners began to gather separately.
Kim Yeong-Man
chose neither the North
nor the South,
but went to neutral India.

From India he went to Mexico.
From Mexico he and others went to Cuba.

In a slum alley in Havana's old town
Ortega Kim
forgot every last word of Korean.
Only the image of his mother in black skirt and white blouse
hung hazily above his eyebrows.

Nam Ja-hyeon

Born in 1872, died in 1933.

Born in Seokbo, Yeongyang, North Gyeongsang province,
she married at nineteen.
Her husband, Kim Yeong-ju,
was killed fighting in Kim Do-hyeon's righteous army.

She remained with her husband's family
bringing up his posthumous child.
When the Independence Movement started in 1919,
she left her remote village,
left her home town
shouting, Long Live Korea! *Manse!*

She was determined to live for the independence of her country

She worked in the kitchen for the Independence Army
in western Manchuria
across the Yalu River.
She quit the kitchen,
made a plan secretly to assassinate the Japanese governor-general.
She failed.

She went to Jillin in Manchuria and continued to work for the
        Independence Movement.
She planned to rescue General Kim Dong-sam
while he was being transported after being arrested in 1931.
She failed.

In 1932 she cut off two fingers
and wrote an independence petition
in her blood,
addressed to the League of Nation's fact-finding commission.

Attempting to murder the Japanese ambassador in Manchuria, she
        was arrested
then tortured severely.
She died in Harbin in 1933.
She was buried in one of the White Russian cemeteries.

No one knows where her child lived or died.

One-armed Park

At dawn on 28 June 1950,
the bridge across the Han River was blown up.
That ear-splitting boom!
Pandemonium.
Silence.
Screams. Groans.

About a thousand
of the Seoul citizens who fled hastily over the bridge
after the war began
died in the explosion.

Among them
a man who lost one arm
grabbed a drifting box with the other hand
and held on to reach the bank at Noryangjin.

He survived,
became One-armed Park, gang-leader of Nampo-dong, Busan,
in 1951, while Busan was the provisional capital.

'Those goddamn bastards escaped first.
After they made broadcast announcements
telling the people of Seoul to stay and not worry,
those goddamn bastards themselves escaped.
The goddamn President,
those goddamn ministers.

'Goddamn military, goddamn whoever.
What?
They were serving the nation?
They called themselves the nation's bulwark?'

One-armed Park spouted abuse as he snuffed the lighter.
The cigarette smoke drifted off. Goddamn!

Yong-sik, Aged Five

Truly his home was poverty itself.
This five-year-old
had moved his lips for half a day.
Does he have a sweet
in his mouth?
Is a sweet melting
in his mouth?

'Say "Ah."
You little rascal, what're you eating?'

He opened his mouth, 'Ah.'
On his little tongue
was a pebble.

He was hungry and wanted something to eat,
so he'd picked up a stone,
put it in his mouth
and was moving it around.

At sunset, as goose-flesh spread wide,
a wind came down from the hills.

After Seoul Was Recaptured

After the three months of the People's Republic,
everything in Seoul was destroyed.
Empty houses and
the houses of those who hadn't left yet,
all of them,
on every rainy day,
echoed with the endless sound of raindrops falling from the eaves.

Those who collaborated during the occupation numbered 400,000.

Sentenced to death,
imprisoned for life,
30 years' hard labour,
15 years,
5 years.

People were arrested after anonymous tipoffs,
rounded up on false accusations.
Ancient enemies
were denounced on concocted charges of being reds.
Kim Cheong-nang in Seodaemun Prison,
sentenced to life in prison,
had a black wart between his two eyebrows
that made him look most solemn.

All he had done was attend one rally
organised by the city communists during the occupation.
He was indicted as the vile instigator of a rally
thanks to the scheming of Yun Min-u, who owed him money.

Tortured, he was dying
of malnutrition,
of depression.

Finally, he died of a stroke
after he'd served only two years of his life sentence.
No one came forward to claim his body.

He was buried on the slopes of Mount Geomdan, Gyeonggi province
in the cemetery for prisoners with no known relatives.

Commie 1

The more remote a village was,
the more the people there used the lunar calendar.
People's birthdays were lunar dates,
ancestral rites were lunar, too.
The year's farming was done by lunar dates:
when to plant barley,
when to plant buckwheat,
when to plant rice
in terraced paddy fields.

In people's memories
every day was a lunar date.

He spoke with a running nose.
His breath
spilled out and dispersed in clouds of steam.

So, on the twelfth day of the sixth lunar month
the People's Army
passed through this mountain village
Someone said they were from the North's Fourth Division.
They reached the hills of Geochang in the north
via Hamyang from Namwon.

Soldiers who looked very young
were carrying submachine guns the wrong way up.

There was no doubt we were in trouble.
Thinking I should escape somewhere
I took the ox from the stable
and went to my in-laws' home in Sancheong.

The Communist army passed through there, too.

I took the ox and came back home.
I swept away the cobwebs,

warmed the room,
dried out the green mildew.
While I was living like that
someone came down from the hills and took me with him.

I carried food up and down mountains until I was caught.
I was sentenced to twenty-five years.
My knee got broken in jail, my teeth fell out.
I tossed the fallen teeth through the bars.
Sometimes I cried.
I was a commie.

Commie 2

I was no commie.
One day I met my kid's schoolteacher
and bought him a drink
in the tavern at the junction.
As we were drinking a measure of *makgeolli*, then another half-
      measure,
the school teacher
praised my kid saying
his grades were so-so
but he was good at stopping kids fighting.

Then, pinching the wrinkles between his eyebrows,
Mr Kim said:

'In future,
the time will come when everyone lives equally well.
The land will not belong to landowners
but to all who farm it.'

I lost all taste for liquor and opened my eyes wide.
Inside the tavern

there was an old woman
and two other drinkers.

A few days later I heard
that a plainclothesman was coming to arrest me.
The village head shook his head:
Strange,
strange.
You're no commie.

I was scared.
I escaped to my wife's home several miles away,
then moved to another house.
I kept moving around,
as I hated being a burden to other people.

Then a man told me he was on his way up into the mountains,
so I followed him.
I was no commie.
Then, eventually,
I became a commie.

From Jiri Mountain I used to look toward home,
longing to go back down.
Longing to go back down.

Commie 3

When I was six,
my maternal uncle
set me behind him on his bicycle
and sped along the new road with poplars on both sides.
That uncle
was my ideal.

Uncle was a university student in Japan.
Uncle passed the higher civil-service exam.
Everyone in the village came to the congratulatory party
at my mother's parents' house.

But my uncle rejected official positions,
went roaming
all the way to Seoul,
to Buan,
to Daegu.

He was arrested at Suwon Station in 1943.
He spent six years in Daegu jail.
Uncle was a socialist.
Uncle was a revolutionary.
I thought about my uncle in prison.
I stopped playing with Bong-Jin, the local landowner's son.
I decided to stop thinking about pretty Suk-Nye,
daughter of the village head.
Instead,
I played with Su-Man and Tae-Rang who were from poor families.
I shared my ration of food with them.
I gave them my pencils.

From the age of 15
I was a socialist like my uncle.

Only nobody
knew that I was a socialist.
At night, alone,
I used to tremble.

Uncle Yu Sang-Seop finally died in his fourth prison.
It was the day after Stalin died.
I burned one of Uncle's books up the hill behind the house.
I cried a lot.
It was where foxes used to cry
but now there were no more foxes.

Lovely Geum-gak

He was such a lovely boy.
It was no surprise that even men,
sighing in admiration,
felt secret passions for him.
Truly,
he was a boy like a spider's web with fresh dewdrops
like a flower's stamen with pure dewdrops,
a boy with the spirit of the point of an arrow flying
He was a young old man
such that no one should dare make light of him.

Living in exile high in Mount Paek-un,
Heobong had a little boy, Geum-gak,
as company for his solitude,.
By the age of ten he was said to have read most books.
Heobong praised him:
'You are truly my teacher,
how could I ever be your teacher?'

At eighteen, that boy was dying of lung disease.
'If heaven grants me a few more years of life,
I would like to read the books I have not yet read
before I leave the world.
What's the use of praying?
Father, mother, do not cry for me,'
and with those words, he closed his eyes.
Should a life be supposed to be long?
Should a life be supposed to be whole
only when it leaves something behind?
Swallows go south leaving nothing.

Headmaster Shin Jin-seop

The headmaster wore round, black-rimmed glasses.
The moustache below his nose
was always neatly trimmed.
He left a dry cough as a sign of his presence
in places where nobody was to be seen.

He had extra time to care for the flowers,
in the school garden
and in the garden in his official residence.
Coxcombs,
four-o'clocks,
asters,
plantain lilies,
chrysanthemums…
the flowers bloomed in harmony according to the season.

One evening
guerrillas came down from the hills.
When they demanded the mimeograph machine,
he said he could not give it to them
because it belonged to the school.
They said that they couldn't help but kill him.
He opened the office.
They carried off the machine.

The next day the police took away the headmaster, his hands tied;
he was guilty of helping guerrillas.
He became a traitor,
a red.
His limbs drooped.
He was beaten with clubs
until nearly a corpse.

He ceased being a headmaster,
became a convict and began a ten-year imprisonment.

What he most envied were those convicts who took care of flowers.
Every day,
they took care of flowers –
dahlias and roses.
The cut flowers were sent outside to be sold.

How he longed to take care of flowers,
just like when he was headmaster.

Yi Bok-nam from Geochang

In January 1951, Yi Cheol-su was fourteen.

His grandmother, Yu Bun-nyeo,
his father, Yi Jong-muk,
his mother, Ms Baek,
his younger brother, Cheol-ho,
the farmhand, Mr Bak,
the maid, Cham-rye with the double-crowned hair,
all six were massacred for the crime of being reds.

However,
Cheol-Su and his younger sister Bok-nam survived,
having gone to their mother's home.

The southern soldiers
dragged ten-year-old Bok-nam off
and drove a nail through her palm
to force her to say she was a red.

'I'm not a red,
I'm not a red,'
she screamed.

Finally,
she said,
'I'm a red,'
and fainted.

The world was frozen.
The sky
was frozen
blue,
deep blue.

Her brother, Cheol-su,
afraid of the world,
afraid of the soldiers,
stole away into the mountains.
Inevitably,
he became a young partisan guerrilla.

In 1956,
nurse Yi Bok-nam of the Red Cross Hospital in Daejeon,
a scar in her right palm where the nail went through, was quiet.
Right-handed as a child,
she was quiet now and left-handed.
She was so good at giving subcutaneous injections
that the patients never knew if the needle was in or not.
When she delivered an injection into a vein
nobody felt the least pain.

Im Chae-hwa

Sadder by far to lose his mother at eleven
than at five.
At five, he wouldn't have known the sorrow.

He grew up on sorrow,
here, on the earth.

Paternal aunt's skirt,
maternal aunt's skirt,
maternal uncle's wife's skirt,
as he grew, he learned that none of those
was as good as his mother's.

In lieu of fertile earth,
he put down roots in rock,
so his life was tough.
The leaves that would dance when it rained
withered.

When he was three,
his father had died.
After that the years were all uneasy.
In January 1951 when he was eleven,
his mother was dragged off to Baksan Valley
and died with the other villagers.
She died without learning why she must die.

The noun 'red' –
a traitor who secretly collaborated with communist guerrillas –
that was all.

A few shards of human bone
no one could tell apart,
whether they were his mother's –
who could never tell A from B –
or someone else's
emerged from the ground.

Twenty-year-old Im Chae-hwa's eyes grew moist.
This world was all wrong.

Township Head Park Yeong-bo

The official name of the Geochang Massacre of the Innocents
was the CheongYa Operation.

Some six hundred people were brought
into the classrooms of Sinwon primary school.
One officer asked if any were families of military policeman.
A few families came forward.
It was true.

A few more families came forward.
This was not true.
They claimed they were MP families
in order to survive.

Then township head Park Yeong-bo stepped forward,
brazen faced,
with a large birthmark on his face.
He dragged one man out:
'You're from no MP family.'
Then he dragged another one out:
'How can *you* be from a policeman's family?'

The six hundred or more townsfolk were bound and taken away.
Gunfire ran out in a gully
beneath a steep hillside.
Then
all was quiet.

Ten years later came the April Revolution.

On the day a cenotaph was to be erected
the families of the victims
went *en masse* to Park Yeong-bo's house.
They dragged him a couple of miles
and made him stand before the graves.

He ran away.
People hurled stones furiously.
He fell as he fled.

One year later came the military coup of May 1961.
People were arrested
for the murder of Park Yeong-bo.

The CheongYa Operation is still on. It's lasted a long time.

A Baby in the 4 January Retreat

On 31 December 1951
President Syngman Rhee reluctantly ordered the citizens of Seoul
       to evacuate.
The Chinese human wave strategy
was once again threatening Seoul.

General Ridgeway, commanding the American forces,
ordered his men to retreat to the south of the Han River.

On 3 January 1951 –
not much of a new year –
the government hurriedly left.
Three hundred thousand Seoul citizens
had to cross the frozen Han River
to head farther
and farther south.

In Waryong-dong, Jongno-gu, Seoul,
one newborn,
the youngest child of the owner of the Seonil Printing Company,
a baby not yet entered in the family register
so still nameless,
was just called,

Dear,
My dear,
My weevil, little rice weevil.

It crossed the Han River ice
on its mother's back

So it began life.
They were lucky. At Suwon they got a ride on a freight train.

A Grandmother

Su-dong's grandmother
who lived below Jinnamgwan Hall in Yeosu, South Jeolla province,
knew exactly how many roundworms
her little grandson Su-dong had in his stomach.

When I'm with my grandson
I can see the camellias on Odong Island;
more than that, I can even see
the camellias on Geomun Island over the sea.

Yeong-u, a refugee child,
was extremely envious of Su-dong.

Ah, if only I had such a clairvoyant grandmother!

The siren of the boat heading for Tong-yeong came echoing.
Or maybe it was the boat *from* Tong-yeong?

Age of Spies

If you did not provide a traveller with a place to sleep,
your family was disgraced.
If you offered cold food
to a traveller,
several generations of your family were disgraced.

Even sixty years ago,
even fifty years ago,
even in days when the nation was stolen from us,
even in wartime,
traces of that old hospitality remained.

Whenever you set off
carrying only a staff and a change of clothes,
each village you passed through
took warm-hearted care of you,
your food and lodging.
If you stayed somewhere for three days, then fell sick,
they'd even provide you with medicine.

Long ago, when Hamel and his companions,
Dutch survivors of shipwreck,
were being escorted from Jeju Island to Seoul
by way of Jeolla Province,
they received a warmer welcome
than they had ever received
in any Christian country in the world.
It was the hospitality given
when humans meet other human beings.
They were moved to say: on our weary journey
the generous hearts of Joseon's people
are incomparable with those of other lands

Some centuries later,
after the war,
that hospitality vanished.

Not only were visitors treated coldly;
people began to report them to the police.

A suspicious person is a spy.
A traveller is a spy.
Anyone loitering at the seaside early in the morning,
anyone who laughs for no reason
at the sight of someone, anyone, all are spies.
Report them.
Report them and earn a reward that will change your luck.

In this country today we have no more wandering travellers.

Two Kilos of Pork

In 1926, Korea's Provisional Government
was being pursued all the time,
starving
as it fled along the shores of the Yangtze River.

Kim Gu, the acting premier,
had abolished things like birthdays long ago.
He was stern with himself:
How can people fighting to regain their nation
celebrate a birthday?

However, Na Seok-ju found out when Kim Gu's birthday was,
pawned his clothes
and bought two kilos of pork.
Everyone cheered up.

With that meat, they were spared for once
their usual poor breakfast.

Kim Gu scolded them:
This will not do.
This will not do.
The Independence Movement knows no birthdays.

Na Seok-ju soon after threw a bomb
that scared the Japanese out of their wits.
He sacrificed himself.
He became a man with no birthday forever.

Manguri Cemetery

The war did not spare even public cemeteries.

The public cemetery in Manguri,
was the underworld of Seoul.
On September 30, 1950,
even that site
became a battlefield.

While six thousand graves lay there,
UN soldiers
and communist soldiers
showered bullets
between the graves,
charged at each other,
stabbed one another with bayonets.

Bodies of fallen soldiers
lay scattered here and there
among the graves.
Bodies of black soldiers,
white soldiers,
bodies of communist soldiers,
were scattered all over the unmown grass.

Seventy-five minutes of deadly battle,
seventy-three dead bodies on both sides:
that was all.

Manguri Cemetery went back to being a cemetery.

3 October 1950

Seoul belonged to the enemy for three months
under the rule of the North Korean People's Republic.
The American air force's bombing raids
went on day after day.
Seoul was reduced to ruins.
Grass grew
between the broken bricks in the ruins.

South Korean troops
recaptured Seoul.
The Northern flag was lowered
from the flagstaff on the Government Building,
the American flag was raised,
followed by the South Korean flag,
and the two fluttered there.

Seoul was under martial law.
Curfew lasted from seven in the evening
until five the next morning,
the time for mice.
Checkpoints stood here and there
in the ruins.
The police who had come back
set about arresting those who had collaborated during the past
        three months,
even children under ten.

The kid of the noodle bar in Juja-dong in central Seoul,
got to know about this harsh world
from early on.
He got to know all about
the world with its beaters-up
and its beaten,
a world where there were thieves
amidst all that fear,
a world where even robbers
and thieves were arrested and beaten with clubs.

He was envious of robbers, envious of thieves.

North Korean Soldiers

North Korean soldiers
who drove south
of the 38th parallel
in the summer of 1950...

North Korean soldiers who supervised night operations on aerodromes.

North Korean soldiers never smoked a cigarette,
afraid of American airplanes:
'The glow of a cigarette can be seen 5 kilometres away.'

They were sixteen,
seventeen years old.

They were carrying submachine guns as tall as themselves.

They had just been mobilised from remote villages.
They were naive,
very shy.

Boys like them were dumped out by the basketful
into the exorbitant war.

Choi Ik-hwan

Everyone was leaving
leaving in a hurry
southward, southward, fleeing refugees
on the 4 January Retreat in 1951,
all but one.

He who refused to leave
had the notion of stopping
this immense calamity,
with his two hands
at any cost
stopping
this war,
a war in which fellow-countrymen were killing one another
left and right
South and North.

Disorder
lawlessness
thieves
ransackers of empty houses
those who had an eye on refugees' bundles
extortionists charged with arresting collaborators
who threatened you with jail
unless you gave up your valuables
absolute confusion
every kind of crime.

After such chaos,
by the end of December 1950
Seoul was utterly empty; everyone had left.

Except one:
Choi Ik-hwan.

Who refused to leave, saying
somehow or other
this brutal game of death must stop.
Choi Ik-hwan.

He remained in his small room
in a shabby house in Seongbuk-dong in Seoul and wouldn't leave,
intending to meet the approaching Northern army
to bring about an end to the war
and persuade the leaders to stop the fighting.
Far from making for Busan
where all were fleeing,
he didn't even head back toward his hometown in Hongseong.

Early in his life
he joined Son Byeong-hui's *Donghak*,
and opened his eyes to the people.
Then he went to Shanghai
with Euichin, one of the last Korean princes,
and took charge of an Independence Movement group,
one known as *Daedongdan*.
After Liberation,
he was a member of the Democratic Assembly.

In January 1951 he did meet Northern officials
and risked his life negotiating a ceasefire.
Starving,
shivering with cold,
suffering from pleurisy,
he never left.

O Se-do the Trader

O Se-do, slightly pock-marked,
accumulated a fortune through brokerage,
all by himself, all of five-foot tall,

with no store,
no office.
Just how rich he was no one knew.
He was considered the richest man in Cheolwon,
the richest man in Pocheon,
in Yeoncheon.
But no one knew just how rich he was.

During the three years of war,
he raked in profits,
crossing the battlefields
to sell things in the North
and in the South,
while the central front repeatedly advanced and retreated,
one hill taken and re-taken
ninety-nine times.

Heavens! More fearful than warfare
were O Se-do's business skills.

At times he dealt in war supplies,
so he had dealings with Yi Sang-jo in the North,
with Jeong Il-gwon in the South.

Sometimes he dealt in military intelligence,
sometimes he dealt with the American Eighth Army.
No one knew who he was.

He had a high-pitched voice,
a sixteen-year-old girl's uvula.
Having a keen sense of smell
he was able to sniff out bean-sprout soup miles away.

A jeep he was riding
got blown up by a landmine.
He was seriously wounded
and taken to the 858 unit's field hospital.
His belt was packed tight with $120,000.

Yeong-ho's Sister

Today is another clear day and in his memory his sister is coming.
Today, too,
in his memory – all he has left –
his sister is coming.

Nine-year-old sister Yeong-seon
and five-year-old Yeong-ho,
the two came down to the South alone.

His sister died,
and Yeong-ho became a combat policeman.
He was ordered to go to Jiri Mountain,
and fought.
While fighting,
he suffered a head wound.

He lost his wits.

His only memory
is the coldest, hungriest, hottest instant
of this present time.
In his memory, all other presents
are dimmer.

He ran away from the hospital.
He stole onto a train and later got off unnoticed.
In the deserted plaza in front of Sintan-ri Station
he was looking for someone, gazing around.
He was looking for Yeong-seon, his sister,
his dead sister.

Yi Geuk-no

After the meeting of the Koryo Communist Party
in Irkutsk
he walked
and he walked,
across Mongolian grasslands,
through sandstorms,
as far as Shanghai in China,
he walked on,
starving.

He walked to attend a secret meeting in Shanghai.
The soles of his feet were black and numb.

So very ardent, entirely devoted to his lost nation.

Hyeon Gye-ok in Shanghai

In 1941 the Shanghai public auditorium looked down on the
          yellowish river.
An international arts festival was being held:
China,
France,
England,
USSR,
Japan.

Inside the hall
each country's flag was hanging.
Outside, too,
each country's flag was fluttering.

Only the *Taegeukgi*,
the flag of Korea, nationhood lost,
was not there.

A young girl, Hyeon Gye-ok,
accompanied an independence fighter
from the French Concession.
As the art festival was ending,
although it was not in the programme,
she suddenly took to the stage
before the emcee could stop her.

After putting up the *Taegeukgi*,
she performed a *gayageum* solo.
Slow, with long breaths,
ardently.
The very rapid *jajinmori* rhythm was entrancing.

The hall sank under deep water.
Applause burst out.

One Chinese spectator wept as he said:
'You have told people from the whole world
of your nation's independence.'

Yi Seung-tae

He was arrested at age seventeen.
He was involved in a plot to blow up a police substation.
Part of the building was destroyed.
He was arrested
as he was making his escape.

After being tortured,
he spent one year in detention before being sent for trial.

His release as a minor was approved.
The detective in charge
ordered him to write in his letter of apology that
when he was released
he would be loyal to the Japanese Empire,
and to seal it with a thumbprint.

'I am a Korean.
I have no duty to serve Japan.

'Once I am out,
I shall fight for our people's liberation
until Japan leaves our land.'

He continued:

'Because of me, my father has become a cripple.
He was stuck in snow
and tortured
to say where I was.
Stricken by frostbite,
he lost one leg.

'So how could I ever be loyal to Japan?'

Young Yi Seung-tae
grew up.
Soon after Liberation
he became deputy head of the youth division
of the Committee for the Preparation of National Foundation.

He was a fine young man.
When Yeo Un-hyeong was assassinated,
he fasted in mourning for one week. Then he disappeared.

Love

I have seen a love that is higher
than parents' love,
than a father's love,
than children's love.

That poem was written by a young man
wandering through northern Manchuria in the autumn of 1930,
fighting for the liberation of his colonised country.

His name, Yi Ik-jae,
aged 27.
He was rather young
to leave such a poem behind.

When he was killed in action,
the South Manchuria independence fighters
buried him at the foot of a hill
and carved that poem
on the wooden gravemarker.

Again
the world went back to parents' love,
went back to wives' and children's love.

And the walls of each house grew higher than the next.

A Single Photo

In August 1950,
as day was dawning,
Shin Jo-jun of Pyeong-san, Hwanghae,
crossed the Imjin River, on the western battle front.
He swam straight across the river
holding in his teeth a single photo
of his mother and father when they were young.

He was in Seoul, capital of the South. It lay in ruins.
Living as a beggar
he became a South Korean.
Then he gave up begging
and ran errands for a grogshop,
then for a shoe-shiner,
bringing him shoes to be polished,
before he became a shoe-shiner himself.

He bought a wooden shack.

Fifteen years after leaving his northern home
he was president of the Actors' Academy in Chungmu-ro, Seoul.
He had his parents' photo enlarged
and hung it on his wall.
Somebody asked:
'What period are those film stars from?'

So-called Student Soldiers

When the Communist army came South,
fourth- and fifth-year middle-school students
were summoned *en masse*
and forced to enlist.

Fourth and fifth years of middle school!

On 4 January 1951,
when the Northern forces came down again,
first-year high-school students
were summoned at random *en masse*:
and forced to enlist.

Boys in their later teens,
those early plums,
those early apples,
those early jujubes

died in battle at Pohang,
died on the central front.

The land the South recovered, wherever the battle ended,
was all graves.

VOLUME 17

That Old Woman

She had many stories in her.
Millipedes dropped from the rotten thatched roof of her hut.
Falling raindrops
were part of her family.

Hard times were her strength.
Neither cholera
nor other common diseases visited her.
Even the ghosts
disliked poverty. The daytime moon was one of her family.

Drinking a cup of water,
she tried to forget a host of stories
in the Japanese colonial period,
when moonlit nights were bright in the ruined nation
and then again in the age of a divided Korea.

Once, Eon-nyeon from the village opposite,
came by after gathering greens and said:
'When you die
we'll make the memorial offerings for you.'
'I don't need that,' she said
with a smile, her first in a very long time.

If she had no teeth
she still had gums.

Her gummy smile was all she had.

Paddy Fields

There were children laughing in the Pyeongtaek fields,
and girls singing, too.
In that hallucinatory world,

there were tender yellow-green
baby rice plants
in the freshly planted paddy-fields.

Now it was the turn of sunlight,
of water.
After three rounds of weeding the rice would ripen.

They were the fields of the Republic of Korea,
fields of the People's Republic,
then of the Republic of Korea again,
then of the People's Republic again,
then of the Republic of Korea again.

After American jets flew over, the fields were quiet.
Don't be sad.
Your descendants will continue forever because of these fields.
The rice is ripening in the scorching heat.

On the dirt bank of one field, homeless dogs are coupling.

Two Deaths

Gwon Pyeong-geun, aged 47.
Yi Seok-u, aged 26.

Gwon put on the suit long left hanging unworn:
now he was a gentleman of the harbor.
Yi appeared wearing a clean shirt
without his usual People's Guard's armband: a lovely young man.

On September 8, 1948
they joined the crowd out to welcome the American military
landing at Incheon harbour,
a zone still being guarded by Japanese police.
There, Gwon Pyeong-geun
and Yi Seok-u were shot dead by a Japanese policeman.

Rejoicing at Liberation,
and gone out to welcome
the liberating army, the allies,
they were killed by the last tatters of Japanese imperialism.
Nay, it was liberation that killed them.

Gweon Pyeong-geun had been chairman of the central committee
of the Incheon branch of the Korea Workers' Union;
Yi Seok-u had been a guard in the people's militia.
Regarding their corpses, the Americans said
that the Japanese police were right to fire.

That evening, the Korea Workers' Union
shouted anti-American slogans
along with anti-Japanese slogans
and tore down from the wall
the Stars and Stripes.

Flowers

In prehistoric times, forty thousand years ago,
as people were moving their homes
one by one from caves to huts,
when a father was killed while hunting
his son
brought him home on his back,
put the body up in a tree
then offered flowers on the ground beneath.

Forty thousand years later
in Jinan, North Jeolla Province,
a family made a grave for a man who died in the war
then a four-year-old boy offered flowers.
Behind him, his mother wept.

A few wild chrysanthemums.

General de Gaulle

Today, again, General de Gaulle was sitting in the café.
The faces around the stove in Café Geosang
behind the old Hwasin department store in Jong-ro, Seoul
turned red
around the hot stove.

His name was Kim Cheol-sun;
his nickname, General de Gaulle;
his occupation, none;
his marital status was unclear –
sometimes he was said to have a son, sometimes not.

More than once every day
the words 'General de Gaulle' were sure to come tumbling
out of his mouth, which looked like a turtle's.

'In France, General de Gaulle got rid of every traitor,
those who fawned upon Hitler,
those who fawned upon the Vichy government.
He executed some,
sentenced others to life imprisonment,
deprived more than 600,000 of civic rights.
But in this bloody Republic of Korea,
pro-Japanese people have become patriots,
while patriots are blamed as traitors,
as reds.
Where on earth is our national spirit?
Of what country is Dr Syngman Rhee president?'

A few days after,
General de Gaulle failed to appear in the café.
An outstanding bill of eight hundred *hwan*
began to gather dust.

Lee In-su

Humanity became a tool of barbarity.
Humanity was a sacrificial offering.
During the Japanese colonial period
talented Lee In-su studied English literature
at the University of London,
then came back. After Liberation
he was the pride of Korea University's English department.

One English teacher from Mokpo,
eager to meet him,
even made the two days' train journey up to Seoul.

Lee In-su was the pride of Korea's English studies,
he looked cool after he'd shaved,
he was laconic at all times.

Lee In-su had a wife and children.
He moved between home and school.
War broke out.
He was not able to leave Seoul.
During the three months under the People's Republic
Kim Dong-seok, who had previously gone North, came back down.
At his urging
Lee In-su made English broadcasts aimed at the American forces.
Even Byeon Yeong-tae, the future premier who had taught English
        in China,
could not match his English.

After Seoul was recaptured
Lee was arrested.
Kim Seong-su, the founder of Korea University,
addressed a petition to President Syngman Rhee.
Many people
tried to save his life.

Defence minister Shin Seong-mo had him swiftly executed.

Lee In-su was a brilliant scholar
when he was in England.
Shin Seong-mo had been a ship's captain amidst wild seas.
He always considered Lee In-su his rival.
From early days,
small Shin Seong-mo
had thought only of getting rid of tall Lee In-su,
by any means.

An Outstaring Game

The meeting started,
the first session of the very long,
very tedious
armistice negotiations.

The UN's chief delegate was American Vice Admiral C. Turner Joy,
the North's was General Nam Il.
Outside Panmunjeom, the fighting was still furious.

Joy proposed: 'Let's make the armistice line the Kansas Line,
passing through Yeoncheon and Cheolwon in Gyeonggi province,
Geumhwa and Ganseong in Gangwon province.'

Nam Il proposed:
'Let's go back to the 38th parallel as before the war.'

Nam Il again:
'During the seven months of the war,
our northern forces occupied territory south of the 38th parallel for
         five months,
while you occupied land north of the 38th parallel for only two months
If you insist on the so-called Kansas Line,
we'll insist on the Nakdong River way down south as the armistice line

166

Joy:
'No. We have gained full control of air and sea.
In the war against Japan
we made Japan surrender
without even one American soldier landing on Japanese soil.'

Nam Il:
'You are forgetting some important facts.
What made Japan surrender
was first the Korean people's fight for independence,
then the Chinese people's eight-year battle against Japan,
and the entry of the Soviet Union into the war.
You fought against Japan for five years,
but you won thanks only to the entry of the USSR into the war.'

After that
they spent the next 7 hours 10 minutes in an outstaring game,
lips tightly shut.
Whoever blinked first would lose.

This scene was witnessed
only by the English interpreter,
second lieutenant Kim Hyeong-gi,
a briefing officer for the defence ministry's information bureau,
and Choi Byeong-u, reporter for the *Joseon Ilbo* newspaper.
All the other reporters depended on Choi.

Later Choi Byeong-u was killed by Chinese gunfire
on the battlefield of Kinmen Island in the Strait of Taiwan.
His wife would become the wife of Professor Wagner
who taught Korean history at Harvard.

Relations in life spread.

A Room at Last

Having escaped, I came back alive.
Grandfather, grandmother,
mother were gone.
I was all alone.
For food, I dug up the roots of *alang* grass,
gnawed pine needles,
ate amaranthus raw.
I lapped up a bowl
of stale left-overs.
I came back alive.
I slept under a straw mat in the shed of some house.
I slept in an empty stable.

I came back to bombed-out Seoul
after it was recaptured.
In Anguk-dong old tile-roofed houses remained,
the houses where court ladies used to live.

There was one house still empty.
I collected scraps of wood and
made a fire to heat the floor.
My body thawed out.
My name is Yi Jong-su.

How long had it been?
Lying on the warmest spot in the room
I looked up at a framed photo of the owner of the house,
who had run away.
A handful of rice remained in a jar.

I ate the rice alone, without side dishes.
I wished
for soy sauce,
I wished
for red pepper paste,

I wished
for aged kimchi.
Saying that, I fell asleep.

Dreams were unnecessary.

Mud-flats on the West Coast

They say Kim Il-sung has come to Seoul.
They say Syngman Rhee is going to Pyongyang.
Who's Mao Tse-tung?
They say Mao Tse-tung has come to Seoul.
Or else
Truman is going to Pyongyang.

They say those goddamn Seoulites
have packed their bags to flee any number of times.
They say all the folk on the mainland
are having a really hard time.

In the most remote of the Gyeongnyeol-bi Islands in the Yellow Sea
live nine fishing families,
and in one of them
is Sujin's Mom,
so gaunt and skinny
she's called 'Bamboo chopstick' or 'Metal chopstick',
with her flat chest.
Today too that Chopstick's been out gathering oysters,
and now she's mending her husband's net,
the net with so many holes.

Three or four times a day
planes pass overhead.
Whether they pass
or not
the waves never stop breaking.

Empty boats creak,
tossing in the waves.

No news at all
from Ilmo's boat,
still not back.
The crimson sun drops down in a flash.
The whole ocean, surprised, grows dark.

If a few planes pass overhead
or not, who cares?

One Day

In the yard of an empty house
a leftist was killing a rightist.

He battered his head
with the back of a spade.
He fell,
his hands bound with wire.

Then he struck his exposed breast
with the back of the spade.
Blood spurted out.

He made his last farewell:
Goodbye, bloody reactionary.

And Another Day

A rightist dragged a leftist
to the square before the station,
and the leftist's wife as well.

You whore,
now watch your husband die.

The first cudgel blow.
A second.
The leftist fell.
A third.
The leftist squirmed.
A fourth.
The leftist lay unmoving.

The leftist's wife, standing stock still,
shed not a tear.

The previous night
she'd been dragged out
and raped by four men.
She shed not a tear.

Old Shin

Let's be off!
Let's be off!

Old Shin, a refugee,
wanted to go back to the home he had left:
216, Sanjeong-ri, Jaseong-myeon, Gujang-gun, North Pyeongan
province.

Half senile and
half insane
he wanted to go back to the home he had left.

Let's be off!
Let's be off!

His son came back, drunk.
Once again he'd had no luck finding a job.

Let's be off!
Let's be off!

His son suddenly shouted:
'You old fool, there's nowhere to go. Drop dead!'

A Simpleton

The living were ashamed before the dead.
The dead were ashamed before the living.

No trains arrived at the station.

The first summer and fall of the war went by.
Winter went by.
The following spring
Yun Do-jun, having survived it all, became a simpleton.

Escaping
        bombing
        killing
        revenge killing
escaping again.

Yun Do-jun, having survived all that,
could not help but become a simpleton.

When children called out: 'Mister Do-jun!'
his eyes were blank.
When children teased him with, 'Hey, Do-jun!'
or with, 'You, Do-jun!'
his eyes were blank.

One child suddenly lost his temper:
'Why didn't this idiot die, why's he still alive?
Not fair! My uncle, *he* died.'

Homecoming

His father's last words:
    Your brother's surely still alive.
    I feel so sad I am dying without seeing him again.
    When your brother comes back,
    tell him that.

Later
    His mother's last words:
    Your brother's coming over the hills;
    hurry up and bring him back.

After Liberation, their long-absent son stood before their graves.
He shed a lot of tears after 29 years.

The anarchist Jeong Hwa-am's homecoming
was a shabby affair.
In socialist society as in capitalist society,
an anarchist must be an object of misunderstanding,
shabbier than a shadow.

Pagoda Park

In Pagoda Park stands the stone pagoda of Wongak Temple
which looks sometimes like an ice sculpture.
It was noisy around that ice sculpture
after the second recapture of Seoul:
a home for the homeless,
a workplace for those with no work.

From mid-morning on
people would gather one by one around the pagoda.
After five in the afternoon
they left one by one.

There was a man
who made a fervent speech there,
holding an old fan,
when about one hundred
or perhaps only twenty had gathered.

He talked about Dangun, our country's founder,
General Im Gyeong-eop,
Kim Jong-seo and
and Han Myeong-hui, politicians in days of old, too.

He looked haggard.
His eyes were not clear and he had wrinkles like a mud-flat.

He said,
'A hundred years from now,
our country will be the centre of the world.
Fifty years from now,
our country will be the top nation of the East.
In future our nation
will receive tribute from 300 countries.'

Kim Dong-bok
never missed a day.
After making a passionate speech for about two hours,
if someone bought him a bowl of noodles
he would gulp down all the broth in a moment,
and then say,
'In future, Korea
will be the presiding country of
the World Presidents' Association.
Wait and see.
Wait and see.
Ah, those noodles were tasteless.'

He misspoke. He meant to say 'tasty'.

He looked around
old panama hats,
felt hats,
helmets,
straw hats,
military caps,
and
bare heads, crew-cuts.

Middle School Classmates

Korea was a battlefield, everywhere.
The battlefront
moved south down the peninsula.
Then the battlefront
shifted north up the peninsula.
The battlefront
left not one place untouched,
rummaged everywhere,
trashed every corner.

Moreover, the battle was not only on the front.
In the rear
between one and another,
there was hatred
deceit,
plunder.

Before, under Japanese rule, foolish people were friends together.
But here on this battlefield
even foolish people turned into one another's enemies.

Yeom Gi-uk informed on Baek U-jong,
saying that he met the younger brother of Kim Chin-gu
who'd gone north after Liberation.
But Kim Chin-gu had already died in the Bodoyeonmaeng *
and his younger brother had gone north, so he'd never met him.
Yeom was Baek's middle-school classmate
but Baek once refused a request Yeom made
so Baek U-jong was denounced.
False or not
if you denounced someone as a spy, you got a reward.
All the guys you disliked were spies.

* After Liberation in 1945 and before the Korean War the South government
tried to convert communist sympathisers; the organisation composed of such
people was called the *Bodoyeonmaeng* (the Bodo League) and most of them
were killed by the police of the Southern government when the South Korean
forces were retreating for the second time on January 4, 1951; that was when
Koreans began killing each other indiscriminately.

Kim Jin-se

His comrades were arrested.
He slipped away to Tianjin, in China,
to a Chinese slum –
the independence fighter Kim Gyu-sik,
together with his wife Kim Sun-ae,
and their son Kim Jin-se.

Neither father
nor mother
taught Korean to their son, born in 1928.

It would mean the end, if ever
a Korean word popped out
while he was playing with Chinese kids.
Agents of the Japanese army
had ears even in the Chinese slums.

Kim Jin-se only learned Korean after he turned thirty.

He learned some very clumsy Korean
from his countrymen in the Korean Provisional Government
in Shanghai,
in Chongqing.

He spoke Chinese far better.

Chwiwonjang in Northern Manchuria

You had to leave in order to live.
A division of the Japanese army in northern Korea crossed the
        Tumen River
on an operation designed to annihilate the Koreans
to the north of the Tumen River
and north of the Yalu.

In revenge for the great defeat at Cheongsan-ri
the Japanese planned an operation with three slogans:
    Kill on sight!
    Burn on sight!
    Rob on sight!

The Koreans in western Manchuria
fled northward,
northward,
to the end of maize fields, millet fields,
northward to the end of the sky.

Following the Songhua River for a hundred *ri*
beyond Harbin,
they fled to the far end of the open plains of North Manchuria,
and there, at the far end of those open plains,
there,
they unloaded,
made dugout shelters, settled down.

Seokju's first words:
    The waters of this Songhua River flow all the way
    from Korea's Paektu Mountain...

They decided to make it the second base for the Independence
      Movement
and mulled over ways to live.
Brothers were warm-hearted toward each other
in their life of exile.
Yi Sang-ryong
and his younger brother
Yi Bong-hui
shared warm affection and
strong convictions.

There, in Chwiwonjang,
the birch-wood fire in the kitchen
never went out
throughout several bitter winter months.

That Year's Paper Korean Flags

Japan surrendered at midday on 15 August 1945.
Called an unconditional surrender,
it was conditional,
for the emperor stayed in place.
From that day
paper Taegeukgis fluttered across the Korean peninsula.
They fluttered there, sometimes just with a yin-yang symbol
and the four divination signs added
to the red circle of a Japanese flag.

On 20 August 1945,
a declaration was issued by the Soviet Army:

We, the Red Army, grant all the conditions
needed for the Korean people
to begin to live with freedom and creativity.
The Korean people themselves
should create their own happiness.

On 2 September 1945
General Order No. 1 was issued from the headquarters of America's
        MacArthur:

All Korean people must immediately obey all orders
issued under my authority.
All acts of resistance to the occupying forces
and disturbances of public peace
will be severely punished.

Taegeukgis that had been hidden since March 1919 were fluttering
        everywhere.
Taegeukgis that had been buried until August 1945 were fluttering
        again.
However, the Americans were not a liberation army
but an occupying army.
Paper Taegeukgis were fluttering for them.

Chin Mu-gil of Yongdun village, Miryong-ri, Mi-myeon, Okku-gun,
        North Jeolla
was good at painting Taegeukgis on paper.
He drew fifty a day.
He even took some over the hill to Okjeong-ri.
He sent some to Mijei village, too.

On 6 October 1945
an American jeep appeared in Yongdun village.
The villagers welcomed the big-nosed soldiers
carrying Taegeukgis in their hands.

Who knew that the soldiers would start hunting women?
All the village's pigtailed young women
hid in fireholes,
crept under the floors,
hid in bamboo groves,
but they were dragged from their hiding places
up the hill behind the village.

In Hamgyeong province in northern Korea, too,
it's said that Soviet troops robbed people of their watches
and hunted for women.

Jin Mu-gil's cousin in Okjeong-ri, a tall girl,
locked herself in her room
and huddled all night in the closet, a cripple, a hunchback.

Exoduses

In January 1911
having lost their nation,
the people left, fleeing from the Japanese:
the first exodus.

In 1912
more people left, fleeing from the Japanese:
the second exodus.

In the summer of 1913
more people left, fleeing from the Japanese:
the third exodus.

And a fourth exodus, fifth, sixth...
during the Japanese invasion of Manchuria in 1931,
even during the Pacific War in 1942.
They left
with one pot,
one blanket,
and a sick child on their backs.
Farmers who for centuries had never once thought of leaving
left.

Tomorrow, when they hope to regain their country,
and today, with its starvation, embraced one other,
and they were hopeless on the long mountain ridges
while the sun set.

Amidst such processions
a boy was growing up
who would later throw a bomb
at the Japanese emperor.
Revering Yi Bong-chang
who was executed after throwing a bomb at the Japanese emperor,
he changed his name from Nam Ji-su to Nam Bong-chang,
made a bomb, and was caught in the act.

A Scene

A little boat was floating on the sea off Byeonsan.
During the war
sun-bronzed Gang Dong-su
put out to sea
to draw his father's spirit out of water.

Bailing out the boat,

>   Father
>   Father
>   Father, come on out.

In the summer of 1950
Gang Byeon-hwan, a guard at the office of the People's Committee
in Buan, North Jeolla province,
was thrown into the sea with all the other red collaborators
as the communists retreated northward.

>   Father, father, don't be afraid, come on out quickly.

That Child

By the sea in Asan,
South Chungcheong province,
rose a hill that looked about to collapse,
a hill
that had thawed after freezing.

Ah, that child,
Kim Tae-seop,
left all alone and
always crying.

A boy in his early teens
with his head completely shaved
passed by some clumps of goosefoot.

Following him
was one hollow-bellied goat.

Not a boat was in sight on the evening sea.
Not a tree on the hills.
His parents, reds, had been arrested and had died.
Their only child
was sent to his maternal uncle's house.

He grew up working in the paddies
and in the fields.
Today
he has walked a long way
and is gazing at the sea.

Of father,
of mother,
no sign.

Chi-sun

The Soejeongji field,
the Bawipaegi field,
the Galmoe field,
the Jaechongji field,
then over the hill, the Bangattal field,
the Bangjuk field.

Work was unending throughout the year.

First daughter, Chi-sun was adept at housekeeping,
a good worker.

Drawing water at daybreak,
cooking,
pounding the mortar,
boiling cattle feed,
carrying food to the field-workers,
sweeping the yard,
removing the ashes,
catching insects in the kitchen garden,
doing laundry,
weaving straw sacks on rainy days,
patching old clothes by lamplight
in the evenings.
She had no time to catch a cold,
no darkness in which to look up at stars.

She wasn't born to be a person,
she was born just to be a labourer.

One wish
lay in her heart:
never to marry
into a household with a lot of work.

Then, thanks to a matchmaker, she married
a son of the miller, of all people.

From early morning,
together with one errand-girl,
she measured out the weight of rice
in the dust-filled mill
and in the evenings
kept watch over the watermelon and melon patches.

She wasn't married as a person
but as a labourer.
Her husband was an invalid,
a consumptive.
She had to prepare drinking tables
for her father-in-law

three or four times a day.
Worn out after such a life, she watched
her husband, his health improving,
take a concubine, a new labourer.

Yi Jong-nak

Intent on restoring Korea's independence by all means,
he went into exile in Shanghai.

One day at dawn, Yi Jong-nak
woke from a dream where families back home
dressed in white were waving their hands.

After that he fell sick.

He went to a German hospital,
to a Japanese hospital.
He did not want to die
in a Japanese hospital,
so he moved to one in the French concession.

One day,
An Chang-ho visited him in hospital.
He told him to believe in Christianity.
Sick, Yi Jong-nak replied
that he could not believe in order to live;
once he got well he would believe with a sound mind.

One day
he said quietly to his comrade Jeong Hwa-am,
'Hwa-am, I'm dying. Go on fighting for me as well.'
Clutching his comrade's hand
he died.

He did nothing really to contribute to the independence movement,
not one act to speak of.

His forearms were so strong an awl could not pierce them.
He was good at the violin, good at sports,
good at singing at drinking parties.
Yi Jong-nak stood briefly on a small corner of his times, then went
away.

The Lock-seller

Even a wooden shack had to have a lock.
Anyone who went to sleep leaving the front gate open was a fool.
Anyone who went to sleep without locking the door to his room
was a fool.
Midsummer evenings,
while people were killing and being killed on the front,
in the rear thieves made their rounds by night.

Everyone had to have a padlock.
Safely locked in,
they had to hear in their dreams
the waves of the night sea.

A dusty wind was blowing in Gongdeok-dong in Seoul.
At the entrance to the alley
a seller of locks and keys
walked by, metal locks jangling from his clothes,
dressed in clothes heavy with clumps of iron.

> Buy my keys!
> Buy my locks!
> Keys repaired. Locks repaired.

> Buy my locks!
> You can trust only to locks.
> Buy my locks, buy my keys!

Two passing middle-school boys asked:

'Hey, Mister!
What's better, keyhole or key?'

The lock-seller laughed.

'Hey kids, I don't know,
go home and ask your parents.'

Yi Yohan the Orphan

Not one child was crying.

On the plaza in front of Busan station in 1952
there were children five-years-old,
six-years-old,
eight-years-old,
and some you could not tell:
five? six? eight?

Some bigger ones were eleven.
Some smaller ones were nine.

The children, wearing old woollen hats,
had been sent from Daegu, were headed
for Zion Orphanage at Songdo, Busan.

Gap-toothed children
deaf children
children with long trails of snot.

When they passed through tunnels
they were covered with coal smoke
in trains without windows

None was crying.

Crying was cowardly. Crying was shameful.
One of those children
was named Yi Yohan.

He had been given the family name of a pastor at a Daegu church.
His Christian name was that of John the Evangelist.

He knew nothing of his mother,
nothing of his father.

Later, this child
grew up to be one of the policemen who opened fire
to suppress the students protesting
in front of the Presidential Mansion
during the April Revolution in 1960.

Police sergeant Yi Yohan.

South Gate Street, Suwon

Soldiers,
gum sellers,
horse-carts,
ox-carts,
piles of droppings in the wake of the carts,
paper-boys,
combs, fine-toothed bamboo combs, glass beads, cheap necklaces,
urchin beggars,
Japanese-era trucks,
American army trucks.

One old beggar lay prostrate all day long.

No sign of human pity anywhere.
The hungry grew hungrier.
The cold grew colder.
In Suwon's South Gate Street,
Myeong-gu
had no shit inside him today as the day before. None.
He could get no food
anywhere round the city gate.

For three *soju* bottles, he could get a few crumbs of bread.
But here there was nothing like that in sight.
Only, only
the world.
Myeong-gu's only thought was for a bowl of rice.

Hey, monks in mountains, what use are those koans you're
        contemplating?

Cheonggye Stream

The clothes they were wearing were American-made,
trousers from relief supplies,
and dyed American military jackets –
but
in the university's French department
students dreamed of themselves as Sartre,
Camus,
André Malraux.
America outside,
France inside.

Perhaps for that reason,
the long Cheonggye Stream
flowing through Seoul between Jong-no and Ulji-ro
was not Korea's Hudson River
but Korea's Seine.

There was the Café Seine in Myeong-dong, too.

The Seine was a place for washing clothes,
the Seine was a sewer
with melon-sized balls of shit floating down.
The Seine was a rubbish dump.
A little farther down the Seine
on the bank toward Gwansu-dong
was Division Four of Cheonggye Stream
where the shanty town began
and battles for survival were intense.

Girls working in clothing factories along Cheonggye Stream
lived in rented rooms in shanties.
The owners were kind-hearted by night,
full of abuse by day.

It was one month since Jo Ok-ja had come to Seoul
as a factory girl.
Every one of her fingers ached.
She worked all day at a sewing machine,
with nothing to eat but five small pieces of bread.
During overtime one night
she felt dizzy, collapsed.

She liked nights.
Sometimes, in her dreams,
she saw her mother.

Heukseok-dong

One dim bulb dangled from the ceiling
of the comic books reading-room.
The shoe store stank of leather.
Flies tended bar, no customers.
In the barbershop, honey soap.
Cheap bread stands.
In the mending shop, an old worn-out sewing machine.

All the way along, nothing but wooden shacks,
steep alleys barely wide enough for one
all the way along

There was a single water tap down below.
People lined up with empty water-cans
and a 10-*hwan* coin; once the cans were filled,
they carried them panting up the alley.

While people were living like this,
on the battlefront people died
and at the rear, people were born.

One woman gave birth two days ago,
and here she was out carrying water.
Her breasts hung
dangling from beneath her blouse.
She gave the child the name
of its father's North Korean home.
Yu Seon-cheon.
Seon-cheon! Seon-cheon!
Our darling Seon-cheon!
A sliver moon rose early
to shine over this slum-village on a hill.

The Porter at Seoul Station

At 5 a.m. the night train from Busan arrived,
an hour after the end of curfew.
He had to be ready at the exit.
Soon the passengers debarked.
The haggling over porterage was brief.
One large suitcase,
one sack of grain,
one small case,
all loaded onto the A-frame,
while the owner followed behind.

He carried the load as far as the bus stop
across the road,
then demanded five hundred *hwan*,
saying the bag was far too heavy.
He refused to put the bag down, demanding payment.
Fingers wagged as they quarreled.

Finally the porter won
after reducing the charge
to four hundred hwan.
No need to be polite, no saying
Thanks or
Good bye.

The porter, Im Ho-sun,
had lost a son the day before.
Today he had come out
and made 400 *hwan* on his first load.
Once work was over at nightfall
he would down a shot of *soju*.
Only then would sorrow for his dead son
come welling up.

Until then
Seoul station spurned sorrow;
at the most extreme moments of life,
sorrow too is superfluous.

The 1920 Massacre

Even in the wilds of Manchuria, their place of exile,
the people from Korea
built schools in their villages.
Teaching their children
was the core of the Koreans' life.
They built houses with floors of clay,
planted maize,
and barley.

After erecting four corner pillars of logs
they covered the roofs with stones packed close like moss
to keep them warm.
The buckwheat harvest was better than the barley.
Even scattered wildly
as if by a mad girl on a seesaw,
it's tough, grows well.

They raised hens, too,
feeding them corn.
In winter, the people had only buckwheat noodles.

At night
a pine root was used to light the lamps.
Tomorrow they would exchange
a handful of corn for a handful of salt.
Their kimchi, unsalted, was tasteless.

At school
they sang the school song.
Instructor Kim Chang-hwan of the Sinheung Military Academy
shouted commands in a voice so resonant
it echoed off the surrounding hills.

They studied Korean language,
Korean history,
Korean geography,

calligraphy,
composition,
singing,
arithmetic, multiplication tables.

All such villages were burned to the ground.
Everyone was killed.
Everything ransacked.
Nobody was left to grind their teeth.

Old Cha Il-man

As the southern forces marched northward,
at Suritjae village on the banks of the Hantan River
one hundred humble thatched houses were set on fire.
All but one man died, leaving a deathly silence.

The one who survived, Cha Il-man, was sick and old.

He took one look at the dead village.

Crawling outside,
he drank lye beneath the wooden step.
His legs soon stiffened.

Nobody remained.
He himself was a word that nobody
could understand.

Hong Jin-su

His nickname was Inchworm.
On weeding days
he said not a word all day.
Some people working alone
mutter and
mutter,
saying things no one can understand.
But Inchworm Hong Jin-su said never a word.
Herons would fly in close, then fly away again.

In February 1951,
shortly before the second draft for the national militia,
the village youths
all drank castor oil to induce diarrhoea.
They had to lose weight.
Under 45 kilograms, they would be disqualified.

Later, however, whether 40 kg or 30,
they all passed the medical exam, second class.
Inchworm cut off the top of his right index finger
with an adze.
He buried the severed fingertip on the hill behind his house.
Within twelve days the finger healed.
Meanwhile he failed the medical, classed third grade.

Relieved, he set about selling tofu.
Putting the tofu trays on his shoulder
he left home early, before breakfast time.
   Buy my tofu.
   Buy my tofu.
He did evening rounds, too.
   Buy my tofu.
   Buy my tofu.

After his parents quit the world
he provided his four younger siblings with food,
fed them as well the tofu that was left unsold.

VOLUME 18

Ong-nye's Husband

Putilovka village in far-away Hassan,
where three borders meet:
Korea, Manchuria, Russia.

In secret, Korean farmers
would cross into that region,
as yet free of bandits.
They built hovels to keep out wind and rain
and survived by grazing cattle and goats
every day on the grass of three countries.
There they lived, snaring birds
on the banks of the Tumen,
catching wild deer,
sowing grain and hunting.

While washing clothes by a stream,
hunter Jang Gil-seong's daughter Ong-nye
met a man on a horse.
His eyes were hollow
with hunger.
He couldn't even dismount by himself
Ong-nye wiped her wet hands and helped him down.
She went back home for some cold rice
and returned to feed him.
A Korean independence fighter,
he had crossed the river
on his dead commander's horse,
pursued by the Japanese.
Actually, he'd rowed across,
the horse swam.
He hadn't eaten for three days.

Ong-nye brought him home.
When her father returned from hunting, she begged:
Let this man become my husband.
Allow your daughter

to become this man's wife,
Father!
Her father Jang Gil-seong
tossed his catch – two cock-pheasants –
at the stranger's feet.

Old Madman

He goes about with a dog's bone stuck in his belt.
He gobbles up earthworms
and frogs, too, all deftly caught
Heuh heuh,
heuh heuh heuh,
he laughs, looking at the sky,
the sky where hawks hover.

Neighbourhood kids
tease him,
throwing stones.
Heuh heuh,
he laughs.

At the sound of a plane he falls flat on his back.
Asleep
under the bridge beyond the village,
his face becomes utterly holy,
utterly peaceful.

When the curs bark at him
he bows his head obsequiously, twisting his hands, saying:
   'I did wrong.
   I did wrong.'

Tae-sun's grandmother explains:
'He's a fellow from Uitteum in Sangchon-ri
who went mad after losing two sons.'

One was conscripted in the Pacific War and never came back.
One was drafted in the Korean War and never came back.

Gunfire in Bongdong-myeon, Wanju

Soldiers of the People's Army
were despatched to every hamlet in the occupied areas.
One soldier arrived in Bongdong-myeon, Wanju, North Jeolla
          province.
A greenhorn soldier, always laughing,
he drank the liquor
that the villagers offered with a village girl,
then went into the bean-field with her.

This became known.
His comrades hastily shot him: no trial, nothing.
After that, not one but three soldiers
were stationed in Bongdong-myeon.

A little later, two left.
The third stayed for the last two months
of occupation, then left.
He never accepted a single leaf of tobacco,
let alone a free drink.
This greenhorn soldier left
firing blanks from his submachine gun.

At the foot
of the village's clay walls and crumbling reed fences
balsam prospered, flowering
no matter who went or didn't.

A Cow in Gangneung, 1953

War
affects cows, too,
dogs, too.

The war
made not just the eyes of humans
but the eyes of animals bloodshot.

During spring plowing,
one cow would not obey.
Urged on:
This way!
This way!
it just flopped down on the ground.
Shin O-man of Gangneung put up with that.

As Shin O-man's son
was pouring out the boiled cattle feed
he was gored
and one horn pierced his thigh.

Shin O-man couldn't put up with that.
With his wooden club.
he gave the cow a blow on the back

War
drives humans mad,
cows too!

He considered selling it,
then, calming down,
decided to wait
a little longer.

Seeing as how the long-drawn-out negotiations for an armistice
are almost over, surely the war is heading away
from our cow, all that we have
and part of the family.

Kim Jong-ho

His mother,
his younger sister,
and his two younger brothers
were caught and killed by the departing commander of the
        People's Army.

Kim Jong-ho, who ran away and so survived,
caught the commander's daughter,
dragged her into an empty house,
raped her, then killed her.

He also caught another commie's wife,
raped her, then killed her.

He killed in that way
three times,
or four,
or five,
then, on a full-moon night,
climbed to a hilltop and wailed.

After that he drank every day.

He smashed the window of the tavern.
He grabbed the bar-girl by the hair and swung her around.
The neighbourhood menfolk
carted him off,
his limbs flailing.

He went away. Somewhere.
His house was sold off.

Sim Bul-lye

The war was over.
The war had lasted three years which felt like thirteen.
The near-empty crocks on the storage terrace made whining sounds.
The blue sky descended
on the soy sauce left in the crocks
and wept salty tears.

Early summer,
on the sixth day of the Armistice,
she appeared at Daejeon railway station
wearing a nylon skirt
and a nylon blouse
she'd been storing somewhere,
and sporting a parasol:
Sim Bul-lye.

Almost all who intended to return to Seoul were back.
Daejeon too had gone back to being the same old Daejeon.
The sky alighted close by.
Sunlight poured down on the parasol,
repaired some days before;
sweat pearled on the young woman's breasts.

Yi Song-won, the boy from Gasuwon
who had come visiting every night in her dreams
no longer visited.
He had come visiting every night
since being killed while fighting in the Iron Triangle.

His mother called a shaman;
only after a costly exorcism
was his soul set to rest.

That day she was off to visit her aunt in Jochiwon.
Her aunt who'd been inviting her at every turn:

'Call on me,
call on me.'
So she set off.

She did the washing, cooked the rice,
finished the sewing, swept the yard,
nursed her father,
drew water at dawn,
drew water at night
Finally, free of housework at last,
she went flying along.

What kind of man did her aunt have her eye on?
She could guess why her aunt wanted her to visit.
She might look young,
but deep inside
she knew what was what.
Sim Bul-lye.

Bak Yeong-man

As a child, he was best at the Thousand-Character Classic.
Ikki eon, ikki jae, on ho, ikki ya...
as he finished the last line of the Classic,
his flushed face looked cute.
Bak Yeong-man,
a boy with a good-looking prick –
like a distended ripe pepper when he pissed.
A boy good at twisting thin straw ropes
like his father,
Bak Yeong-man.

In the war he lost a leg.
Field hospital, then
military hospital.
After a long fight,
at the end of long treatment,
he returned to his hometown
with a false leg,
on a crutch.
His neighbours threw a party for him
with *makgeolli* and dried fish.

The barley fields were the same as before.
The mill was gone,
the miller's daughter Sun-yeong was gone.
They said she'd married a refugee from Seoul.
Damn it!
By the time he'd smoked two cigarettes, he'd got used to despair.
He relieved himself.

Seok Nak-gu

Old Syngman Rhee was quick to run away.
He left Seoul in secret
a day ahead
of American ambassador Muccio.
In the official residence of the governor of South Chung-Cheong
         province,
Rhee ate buckwheat noodles
with his wife Francesca.
His face was contorted.

Once Suwon was threatened
he left Daejeon
for Daegu.

He had been the first to run,
leaving everyone in Seoul behind.
He fled, deceiving the people into thinking
that the President was still in Seoul.
Is that how he did things during the Independence Movement?
He hated the insecurity of Siberia,
Manchuria,
and China.
He sought out safety with wealthy America.
If you talked about that carelessly,
the bar owner reported you as a red.
Dragged away by Counter-Intelligence,
soon you couldn't walk.

Drunkard Seok Nak-gu
was sentenced to three years in prison,
three years confirmed on appeal,
reduced to two-and-a-half by the highest court.
His daughter lost the offer of a job she had got.
Her engagement, too, was broken off.

Outside, night rain grumbles.
Inside, Seok Nak-gu grumbles:

In Hawaii, old Syngman Rhee collected donations from the Korean
        labourers.
He easily earned honorary degrees from prestigious universities.
Wherever he went, he created factions, dividing the Korean
        community.
That old scoundrel!

Street Broadcaster Choi Dok-gyeon

One day in late June when it rains often,
at Seoul Radio Station under the People's Army,
the president of Korea University, Hyeon Sang-yun,
the novelist Yi Gwang-su,
the assemblyman Jo Heon-yeong,
all having failed to escape from Seoul,
made broadcasts denouncing Syngman Rhee:

'The South's puppet clique is doomed.
The South's reactionary leader Syngman Rhee should kill himself.'

'Daejeon is still Republic of Korea territory,'
the novelist Choi Dok-gyeon declared,
countering the broadcasts from Seoul
with streetside broadcasts and posters.
Making street broadcasts,
he travelled beyond Daejeon southward
to Nonsan, Iri, Jeonju, Gunsan,
and as far as Mokpo.

Much of the time, he walked;
if he found a friendly truck he would ride.
'Our ally in freedom, the American Army is coming.
Take heart.
The invasion by the Kim Il-sung faction will soon be repulsed.
Don't believe the broadcasts from Seoul
by leaders who have sided with the reds;
they speak under duress.'
When he returned to Daejeon,
after having made it all the way to Mokpo, to Songjeong-ri,
Syngman Rhee had quit Daejeon
and moved to Daegu.
When he arrived in Daegu,
Syngman Rhee had made a detour
and gone down to Busan.

Choi Dok-gyeon, the author of *Sorrowful Song of a Buddhist Temple*,
the dandy Choi Dok-gyeon
travelled on, soaked in sweat, hoarse with broadcasting.

Busan was the last remaining tip of Korea.
He stared at the sea off Taejong Cape.
His street broadcasts were done.

He went back to being a first-class lecher, a second-class journalist,
and a third-class writer.

Gi-seon's Mother

Gi-seon's mother in Gunsan's Oryong-dong wore loose working trousers
from the day she got married.
She had to patch the worn knees
over and over again.
She was fully accustomed to poverty.

Yu Sang-ho's family, five refugees from Jangyeon in Hwanghae
province
were living in the barn of Geum-sik's house.
The wife had to support her sick husband
and three kids.

Buying plaice, sole and other kinds of fish wholesale
and putting them in a rusty tin washbasin,
she went around village after village selling them.
Times she came home with fish left in the basin.

She was always starving.
The traces of beauty in days gone by
were all faded, withered.

Gi-seon's mother went to the kitchen,
prepared a meal with the rice she was so frugal of
and served it with kimchi on a cheap tall serving tray.
She also gave her some barley
in exchange for three of the unsold fish.

Poor people must look after poor people.
Who else will?
Saying that, Gi-seon's mother gave that refugee wife a comb.
If you comb your tangled hair
your parting will look nice, she said.

Page from the Diary of a Youth Who Butt-flogged Kafka

Today is the eighth anniversary of the start of the Korean War.
It's also my big brother's seventh death anniversary.
Eight years since the war started
and in South Korea today there's no right wing,
only the extreme right wing.
In the eyes of the far right
everything's ultra-left.

Dogs are reds, pigs are reds,
even ghosts are reds.

The Armistice Line is still a battle line.

Land of ever-unchanging far right.

In this country
you're not allowed to sing about red flowers.
You're not allowed to paint red sunsets.
My blood is definitely not red.

A red skirt received as war relief
must be dyed black before you wear it.

In the summer of the eighth year after the war started,
my friend became a poet.
He recited a poem about snow glowing white
Another friend had his first exhibition of paintings,
composed entirely of abstracts in black and white.
He trembled at the very thought of pink.

The anti-communist league must be getting bored.
They say one of the league's top executives
shouted in a bar:
Something must happen.
We must make something happen!

I've thrown out Kafka.
Oppose communism.
Eradicate communism.
Conquer communism.

I must join the anti-communist league.
Then I'll be more confident,
for the world will be mine.

Within a few years
I must get promoted, become one of the league's top executives.

I've thrown out Kafka.

Yeong-seop's Mum

The earth keeps sufficient women alive.

War.
Massacres by rightists and leftists.
You who survive
must erect walls of straw mats on the ashes
and begin life again.
You need to set up a rice-cauldron.
You need to make bitter smoke rise up
like the sound of crying.

Cauldrons have been women's work for centuries.
Mulberry trees have been women's work for centuries.

There have to be women.
Only if there are women
can the empty places left by the dead
be filled with new-borns.
Only if there are women
can the stupid men,
when they return home weary of the rough world,
find strength to go back into the world.

After Yun Seong-su's wife lost her husband
she remarried before the three years' mourning were over
and became the wife of Hwang Yeong-mo.
A baby was born at once.

The kids from her first husband
were Min-gu
and Sang-gu.
Then the newborn arrived
and she became known as Yeong-seop's Mom.

Amidst utter poverty she was always brimming with energy.
That was lucky.
Just after Yeong-seop turned one
she got pregnant again.

From the end of dawn until midnight
she was out in the fields,
or hulling barley in a mortar
then she had to go and pick mulberry leaves
and after mulberry leaves
she would pick mulberries and give them to Yeong-seop.

She would walk twenty *li* to market and sell greens
then buy shoes for Min-gu
and Sang-gu.

On the way back home
her breasts heavy with milk, she would hurry along.

Baby must be hungry.
Her whole body soaked in sweat.
What black eyebrows she had!
Just like charcoal.

From behind, the other women would joke:
she's walking fast as a mule
because she wants to hug her husband.
From ahead, Yeong-seop's Mum replied briefly:
I have to nurse the baby first,
then hug hubby or swallow him.

A Mouse

After the bombing
a gaunt mouse came along.
He was glad.

'How hungry you must be!'

Legless Gi-cheol threw his wooden pillow,
knocked the animal senseless,
cooked and ate it.
He cooked and ate the scream the mouse made
as it died.

When would the war end?

The Fiancée

Kim Sin-ok got engaged to Bak U-hwan
although her family objected.
If he goes off to war he's dead.
You want to get spliced with him?
They got engaged regardless.

Because her second brother Sin-jeong
had been killed at the battle of Waegwan
or the battle of Yeongcheon, they reckoned
anyone joining the army was on his way to the other world.

Since they were engaged
their parents
and the couple met
to eat beef broth together in a local restaurant.
Bak U-hwan presented an 18-carat gold ring,
Kim Sin-ok bought a Seiko wristwatch.

Bak U-hwan visited Sin-ok's house
and greeted his future father-in-law, mother-in-law,
then exchanged a few words in Sin-ok's room, no more;
they had not yet once held hands.

She never wore her engagement ring.
The watch stayed in his inside pocket.
As Bak U-hwan was on his way back home
the sound of a jet plane swept the ground.

The day he joined his regiment
he was wearing a good-luck charm belt over his shoulder.
They went to Gang-gyeong station.
Both sets of parents saw him off
while Sin-ok waved standing behind her parents.
She felt shy and sad.

Two years later
on February 5, 1953,
Bak U-hwan came back home in Sin-ok's dreams.
Joyful laughter.
The following day, February 6, he likewise came home.

One month later notice came from army headquarters that he had
        died in action,
with a letter of condolence from his commanding officer.
Next a box containing his remains arrived.
The vice-mayor put on a black tie and came
to offer his condolences on the death of private Bak U-hwan.

Sin-ok stopped eating.
Her drunken eldest brother shouted:
Stupid girl! Now what will you do?
I don't want my sister to live as a widow.
Hurry up and find yourself a husband.
Stupid girl!

VOLUME 19

Orari

Three members of the punitive force in Jeju Island got bored.
They flicked cigarette butts.
They spat.
They called out old Im Cha-sun
who'd been caught in Orari village:
'You, old man, come out!'
They called out his grandson, Im Gyeong-po:
'Come out!'

'Slap your grandfather on the cheek.'

His grandson refused.
They kicked him hard.

'Come on, Gyeong-po, hit me, come on hit me.'

His grandson slapped his grandfather in the cheek.

'Slap him harder, kid.'
They kicked the grandson.

The boy slapped his grandpa hard.

'Old man, hit your grandson.'

This time the grandfather hit his grandson.
Then the old man got punched and kicked by the men around.

'You bloody old red,
slap him hard.'
He slapped his grandson hard.

Grandfather and grandson,
weeping,
hit each other.

The red grandfather
slapped the red grandson,
the red grandson
slapped the red grandfather.
See? These are red games.

Then there was the sound of gunfire.
Grandfather Im Cha-sun
and grandson Im Gyeong-po
could no longer hit one another.

After the gunfire
there's no knowing where the crows of Jeju Island went flying.

One Rubber Shoe

On a sandbar in Miho Stream
one rubber shoe that came floating down
got stuck
and stopped.

The fields along the Miho Stream seemed abandoned and empty.

Who knew
it was the shoe of Ha In-ae, a pretty girl from Yongin?

Who knew
it was the shoe of the dead Ha In-ae?

When she walked under her sunshade,
soon enough
her breasts got moist under her one-piece dress,
from this house and that
men's noses would come out sniffing.

217

Who knew
it was the shoe of Ha In-ae who hanged herself
after being raped by Jeong Deok, a senior officer,
that summer under the People's Republic?

Kim Seong-ju

Oaths made by slicing palms with a knife-tip
and mingling the blood.
Oaths made by each cutting off a finger
and burying the two fingers together.
Through such blood oaths, men of old
used to inscribe heroic aims in life.

Blood oaths could become blood betrayals,
and the two would be estranged forever;
sometimes one killed the other,
was killed by the other.

It happened to the men of ancient times,
to men of the Middle Ages,
to men of modern times.

Kim Seong-ju of the North-West Youth League
and Mun Bong-je were great friends.
Even though they made no oath in blood,
they did go up Mount Namsan, take an oath in liquor
and smash the glasses:
'If you die, I die too.'

As for their loyalty to Syngman Rhee,
Kim Seong-ju was the more vehement,
and Mun Bong-je lagged behind.
When the allies recaptured Pyongyang,
the Americans appointed Kim Seong-ju, of all people,
governor of North Pyeongan province.

Later Kim Seong-ju dropped out
and Mun Bong-je swam upstream like a fish.
What happened?
Unexpectedly
Kim Seong-ju, in a fit of pique, became election manager
for Cho Bong-am of the Progressive Party.

For that, Syngman Rhee detested Kim Seong-ju more than anyone.

On June 25, 1953,
the third anniversary of the outbreak of war,
Kim Seong-ju was arrested by the military police.
Allowed no family visits,
he was killed by the military police
under the command of Won Yong-deok.

He was killed under Martial Law,
by authority of the recently enacted National Security Law
on the fabricated charge that he had conspired to assassinate the
        president

Kim Seong-ju's path was that of the first Republic of modern Korea.

The Younger Brother Stayed Behind

In July that year
the People's Army came down like a torrent,
from Hongcheon to Wonju, from Wonju to Yeongcheon.

Refugees came streaming down, too,
with a pot, some bowls,
a bag of rice, a bottle of salt.
In every village they passed
the villagers killed cows or pigs and sold the meat.
The village people also sold
their belongings one by one.

In any case, the livestock would soon be requisitioned
or carried off by the army.
So they killed them and
received 5 *won* for a pound of beef,
2 *won* for a pound of pork.
They boiled them in soy sauce and sold that, too.

Gu Bon-yeong from Yeongcheon
killed two pigs
and sold them to the refugees.
He sold his goats and killed chickens to sell them, too.

Having sold everything
Gu Bon-yeong himself had to flee southward
seven hundred *li* downstream
along the Nakdong River,
ending up in Busan.

Gu Bon-yeong's younger brother, Bon-ho, stayed behind.
'You leave, Brother,
and take Mother,'
he said; 'I must stay.
If the People's Army arrives,
I'll live in their world,' he said.
'If the Southern army arrives,
I'll live in their world.'

His married elder brother had taken the land
their father inherited, fields and paddies.
Bon-ho was an old bachelor with nothing.

He could live with nothing, he said,
in whatever world he found himself.
That old bachelor Bon-ho
followed the People's Army when they retreated.
Nobody in his family thought he would turn up one night
in their home as a spy.

Little Cheon-dong

In the backcountry of Sangju at the foot of Mount Sobaek
lay a village
of only eleven households.
It was a remote village,
with neither right wing nor left.

Because the world refused to stay still,
these villagers too
followed the head of the neighbouring village, just over the hill,
and joined the refugees on the road.

From the start they had hard times.
Looking back after setting off,
already their houses and their village
looked far away.

Carrying half a sack of rice on his back,
a man dragged along two goats.
The older child carried the bedding,
the younger something lighter.

His pregnant wife went into labour.
Screaming on the grass by the hill path,
she frightened the goats she'd been dragging along
and gave birth to a blood-covered baby.

The man set up a cauldron so she could eat seaweed soup.
He named the new-born Cheon-dong,
meaning 'live a thousand years'.
The baby's left hand had six fingers,
so he tied the fifth and sixth together with thread.

There was no going back.
Mother and child spent a while
in someone's draughty back room.

Then when the People's Army was near
they took to the road once again.
Cheon-dong was lucky:
his mother was healthy and brimming with milk.

Kim Jin-yeol

War made a person swell up
into someone totally different.

In the train of refugees
he stole
five wristwatches
two gold turtles
twenty-four gold buttons
three gold hair-pins
eight gold rings
and seven thousand won in cash.
He was so delighted he whistled, which tickled his ribs.

He approached a sleeping woman who had a fox-fur muffler
and stealthily removed the muffler from around her neck.

He approached an old man driven into a corner by people's pushing
and took the bundle he was clutching as he slept.
Inside he found some cash
and several house deeds.

Amazing!
There are guys who get rich even while they're fleeing for their lives.

How amazing!
Once safely settled in some unfamiliar city,
he fooled a woman into becoming his wife.

Kim Jin-yeol,
son of a stationer at Uljiro 3-ga, Seoul.
Before he fled South,
he had never stolen,
had never looked at a woman.

Bak Gwan-hyeok

Only once did he do good.

Jin-Su's father was
a miser all his life,
a bully all his life,
a liar all his life,
always abusing and exploiting.

Old Bak Gwan-hyeok.

But as he lay dying, at the age of seventy-seven.
he called for his farmhand Myeong-gu.
From his lips issued these words:
'You are my son by our kitchen maid.
The half-acre of paddy over in Jindong is yours.'

Then he spoke to his eldest son,
Jin-su:
'Myeong-gu has our blood in his veins.'

That ruthless old man
had survived in safety
even under the Communists.

Arrowroot-vine sinews his whole life long.

Yi Yeong-geun

In the days of the Liberal Party
he was arrested by Counter-Intelligence.
You bloody red!
Agent for Kim Il-sung!
Agent for Jo Bong-am!
Bastard!
You wretched liberals,
how dare you say anything against His Excellency Syngman Rhee,
you bloody reds!

For one full week,
for all but three or four hours a day,
he suffered
every kind of torture.

Enough to bring Ulsan Rock on Mount Seorak crumbling down.

Through torture
torturers get to know through and through
the one they are torturing.
They got to know that most manly of men,
that most human of humans,
that most admirable man, Yi Yeong-geun.

Baaastard! Fine fellow! Human of humans!

He framed the founding declaration of the Progressive Party.
He followed Jo Bong-am, its leader,
and was close to Bak Jin-mok.

Before Jo Bong-am was arrested
Yi Yeong-geun urged him
to go into exile in India:
he'd arrange for a ship to smuggle him out.

Two days later Jo Bong-am was arrested.

Jo Bong-am was executed.
Yi Yeong-geun, most human of humans,
left for Japan in a smuggler's boat.

His horselaugh was loud.
His inward heart was deep.
He never spoke of past pains
or present poverty.

By himself, alone, he preserved the world of comrades and old
        friends.

Gamak Valley

During wartime the men die,
the women survive.
Cockerels have their necks twisted and die,
hens sit on eggs.

At Gamak Valley in Yeonsan,
north of Nonsan in South Chungcheong
sharp hills
approach the ridges of Mount Gyeryong.

Fifty men died there, once,
while two men
twisted their hair into topknots and revered Kim Il-bu's esoteric
        Jeongyeok.
The small room, the door of which is never opened
was pitch dark even at midday.

Yeonsan's Gamak Valley.

Some forty women survived:
old widows,
young concubine widows,
young widows,
old maids.

If an unfamiliar man appears, their eyes light up.

They each offer a gourd of water with a willow leaf on it.

'You must be thirsty.'
'You look thirsty.'
'You're thirsty.'

The woman from Buyeo with long cheek-bones,
hastily comes forward.

'Drink this water.
I have no idea who you are or where you are from,
yet your face looks familiar.
If you are hungry
I will warm some cold rice, so you can eat before you go on.'

The woman from Ganggyeong poured the water out of her gourd,
grumbling:

'Yesterday she was making up to a male dog,
today she's clinging to a man instead of a beast, that slut.'

One Schoolgirl's Life

Jo Eun-seon,
Jo Sang-yeon's sister in Sinchon,
was so pretty, always quiet and bright
like a rising moon, like moonlight.

Each of the five stalls in the toilets in Sinchon primary school
had the following graffiti:

Jo Eun-seon's mine.
Jo Eun-seon's xx is gold-rimmed.
I want to suck Jo Eun-seon's milk.
Jo Eun-seon is xx
Jo Eun-seon's my wife.
Jo Eun-seon's the sun of our nation.

That Jo Eun-seon was in fourth year of teachers' training college.
Her brother
served as vice-chairman of the local People's Commission.

After the reds withdrew,
she was arrested
and raped by the head of public security.
When the police came in,
the police lieutenant raped her.
The constables
raped her.
Several more people
raped her.
Then
she was buried alive.

Thus ended a schoolgirl's life.

Today's Meal Table

Shin Jang-heon, in his shirt-sleeves,
unfolds the morning paper wide.
He deplores the news, his laments ready-made:

'Fighting breaking out again... the world's going to the dogs, to the
        dogs...'

Where did he learn
that the world cannot be made of peace,
that the world cannot be made of love,
that human goodness is all lies,
that human evil alone is not a lie?

'The world's going to the dogs, to the dogs....'
'The world is all made up of thieves.'

At the table, lamenting, he had three glasses of wine.
On the front page: twenty-one enemy soldiers killed in combat in Inj
Page three: smuggling organisations rounded up in Busan, Masan,
        Yeosu,
and, oh, one mutilation murder.

Han Jae-deok

During the Japanese colonial period
he studied French
at Waseda University, Japan.
He was mad about André Gide:
La Porte Étroite
Symphonie Pastorale.
Then
he fell for socialism,
a requisite for students studying abroad.

On October 14, 1945,
a welcoming ceremony was held for General Kim Il-sung
in Pyongyang's Municipal Stadium.

Two days before,
on October 12,
for the very first time, he proposed to call
Kim Il-sung General Kim Il-sung.
After Han Jae-deok made this proposal,
Kim Il-sung
became known forever
as General Kim Il-sung.

He was always boasting that
he was the one
who made Kim Il-sung a general,
he, Han Jae-deok.

Shortly after the war, Han Jae-deok came South.
He wrote 'I Accuse Kim Il-sung'
and took charge of theory for the South's anti-communist
            movement

He was stoutly built.
If he had met the heavily-built journalist Cheon Gwan-u
they would have vied with one another,
calling each other 'Younger brother', 'Older brother'.
He was just as dark and stout.
In the fifties,
and after that
in the sixties,
in the seventies,
in the eighties,
in the nineties,
he grew old embodying eternal anti-communism in South Korea.
He was dark and stout.

Tachihara Seishu

The thirty-six years under Japanese rule were long for some people.
Short, for some people.
During that time
there were people who were opposed to Japanese imperialism.
There were people who were obedient to Japanese imperialism.
During that time
there were people who enjoyed prosperity under Japanese imperialism.

During that time
there were people
who became completely Japanese,
who deeply worshiped Japan
and Japanese culture.
There were people who every day
forgot completely that they were Koreans.

In Korea, the novelist Yi Gwang-su declared:
'Koreans should be Japanised
so that when you prick a Korean's brow with a needle
you find Japanese blood oozing out.'
In Japan, longing to be Japanese,
he wore Japanese costume and clogs
even when he was alone.

The Japanese novelist Tachihara Seishu
had six different names
in his not-so-long lifetime.

Born in Daejang-dong, Seohu-myeon, Andong, North Gyeongsang,
          Korea,
his name in the family register was Kim Yun-gyu,
which he used for a while
after he went across to Japan.
His new name there was Nomura Shintaro,
or Kim Ingkei,
the Japanese pronunciation of his Korean name, Kim Yun-gyu.

He became Kanai Seishu when he had to be renamed under
        Japanese rule.
After marrying a Japanese woman
he took his wife's family name and became
Yonemoto Seishu,
while Tachihara Seishu
was his pen-name as a novelist.
He was officially authorised to register his Japanese name
two months before his life ended.
Then he died.

Born
on January 6, 1926,
his father was Kim Gyeong-mun, a labourer at Bongjeong temple,
in Mount Cheondeung in a valley near Andong
and his mother was Gwon Eum-jeon.
Before Yun-gyu was born
his father had a son
with another woman, Gyu-tae,
whom he entered in the family register with Gwon Eum-jeon as
        the mother.

When his father died
his mother moved into the town,
then moved far away to Gumi.
From there she crossed over to Japan.
She began a new life in a Japanese slum.
Kim Yun-gyu
went to a commercial high school in Yokohama,
dropped out of Waseda University,
and made his debut as a novelist.

Then his fabrications began.
After the annexation of Korea by Japan, he said,
when the Japanese state policy made Korean noblemen
marry Japanese women,
his father married a Japanese woman.

He was born in the home of his mother's Nagano family,
in Daegu, North Gyeongsang,
on January 6 1927, the second year of Showa,
but the birth date shown in the family register
was January 6 1926, the fifteenth year of Taisho.
His father was Kanai Keibung,
his mother Nagano Ongko.

At the end of the Joseon dynasty, his father,
born into the noble Yi clan,
was adopted into the Japanese Kanai family.
He served as a soldier, then was discharged.
Since he disliked the world
he eventually became a Zen monk.
While residing at Bongseon temple
on the outskirts of Andong,
he used to come down from the temple once a week.

After his father died
he moved into Andong town.
He attended the Japanese primary school for a time
before transferring to Andong ordinary school for Korean children.

When his mother
remarried into the Japanese Nomura family of Kobe,
he was entrusted to a maternal uncle,
Nagano Tesso, a medical doctor.
He went to Japan
and lived in his aunt's house in Yokosuka.
There was Yonemoto Miseyo,
a girl one year below him in Yokosuka middle school,
who was to be his future wife.

He stabbed a student
four years older than himself.
His admission to the school was cancelled.
He transferred to Yokosuka Commercial School.
He attained third grade in *kendo*.

He stayed in Fukuoka at the invitation of his uncle Nagano,
who had moved to the medical school of Kyushu Imperial University.

In the 18th year of Showa, after four years' preparation for the
    entrance exam
he entered the preparatory course at Keijo Imperial University, in
    Seoul.
Then he went back to Japan.
Thus far all pure lies.

Entered law school, Waseda University.
Mobilised into the labour force during the war.
Married.
Was registered in the register of his wife's Yonemoto Family.
Had a son and daughter.

Became a writer.
Received the Naoki award.
Wrote many novels,
many short stories.

A man desperately devoted to Japan, the exploiting nation.
A man so infatuated with medieval Japan
that he transformed himself into a medieval Japanese.
A man of fiction calling himself a descendant of nobility,
half noble by blood.

For him Korea did not exist.
At fifty-four he died of oesophageal cancer.
A rare fellow…indeed!

Sang-gwon, Only Son

Venus assaulted the moon.

The People's Army came down.
The South Korean army moved up.
The Chinese forces came down.
The People's Army came down.
The South Korean army moved up.
The UN forces moved up.

The armistice line was drawn following the 38th parallel.

One village in Maseok, Gyeonggi province, was almost completely
        deserted.
All that remained were some maize stalks
and an elderly couple.

They had no news of their son Sang-gwon
who had gone off as a volunteer soldier.

He was good at painting playing cards.
When he painted a portrait of President Syngman Rhee
in third year of middle school
he received a commendation from the provincial education office.
When the communists arrived,
during the summer when he was in the fourth year,
his portrait of Kim Il-sung was hung on the wall
of the local office of the People's Committee.

Sang-gwon didn't come back.
Even if he had,
since he had painted the portrait of Kim Il-sung,
he could not live.
There was no news,
no news at all,
of their only son.

Ten Days on the Continent

In 1921, the Pan-Pacific Conference was held in Washington DC,
     USA.
In response, Lenin held the Conference of the Oppressed of the
     East in Moscow, USSR.
The Korean Provisional Government in Shanghai was stagnant,
     split into factions.
To escape this gridlock,
some took the Trans-Siberian at Harbin.
But Yeo Un-hyeong, Kim Gyu-sik and others
left from Zhangjiakou, Beijing,
by way of Kulun in Mongolia,
arriving at Kyakhta on the Soviet border.

After twenty thousand anti-revolutionary White Russian Tsarist
     troops
led by Baron Ungern-Sternberg had been completely destroyed in
     Outer Mongolia,
the whole of Outer Mongolia, from which the Chinese were
     banished,
fell under the control of packs of mounted bandits.

The Korean exiles prepared fur clothing, leather clothing,
boots lined with camel fur,
hats made of sheepskin,
overcoats of animal skins,
celluloid glasses
with frames of furred leather,
sleeping-bags made of old sheepskins,
and supplies of dried mutton,
rifles and pistols.
For ten days they traversed the Mongolian desert.
Minus twenty Celsius.
They arrived at their destination after camping out often in the
     open desert.

Along the way they caught a sheep
and boiled it in an empty oil barrel.
Even without salt it made a feast.
By way of towns in Mongolia
by way of Sapsk and Udinsk,
eating frozen black bread cut with an axe,
and by way of Irkutzk,
they finally reached Moscow on January 7, 1922.

China, Mongolia, and post-revolution Soviet Union too, all were
        in utter poverty.
They listened to Zinovyev's speech at the Third International.
They met Lenin,
Trotsky.
Yeo Un-Hyeong emphasised that
the Korean revolution should be carried out
by supporting, encouraging, and correcting the Provisional
        Government,
and that, since Korea was an agrarian land with no knowledge of
        communism,
nationalism should be stressed
and the first objective should be reaching the farmers.
Lenin expressed deep interest in liberation from colonial rule.

Somehow it all seemed so simple.

Yi Jang-don's Wife

On January 10, 1951,
amidst the chaos of flight,
on January 25, 1951,
amidst the final chaos of flight
markets were still open.
So long as anyone was alive
markets opened.

In Seoul, once again in the hands of the People's Army,
so long as anyone at all was around,
markets were still open.

Here and there in the ruins
rice-cakes,
noodles,
makgeolli were for sale.
And bundles of firewood.
And old clothes taken from empty houses.

Even though the bodies of those killed by strafing
lay sprawled in the snow fields,
a market opened nearby. Chickens for sale.

Three-storey houses,
two-storey houses were bombed,
while low single-storey houses survived.
The People's Committee of Seoul City
began work
in City Hall.
Yi Seung-yeop,
swarthy and with a broad laugh,
came back and presided.
Rallies were held
on air-raid-free evenings
in the City Hall Plaza,
where pools or rainwater formed in bomb craters.

Henceforth, the heroic People's Army
will never again make a strategic withdrawal,
and so on.

And during those rallies
here and there around the Plaza,
rice-cake,
noodles,
makgeolli were being sold.

After Seoul was first recaptured
Yi Jang-don's wife,
a strong woman,
sold rice-cakes in the Republic of Korea;
after the retreat
she sold rice-cakes again in the People's Republic.

Sure enough, in 1953, after Seoul was secured,
she made her way into Nagwon-dong, Seoul
and opened the Obok rice-cake store.
A woman
who always wrapped her head in a towel.
A woman
who never so much as blinked during air-raids.
A woman
who knew nothing of fear, or of anxiety.

A Birth

On the night of January 3, 1951,
flames rose high
all over Seoul:
flames from burning military supplies,
flames from burning food stocks,
flames from burning documents.

On the morning of January 4,
low-flying aircraft
made an announcement from loudspeakers:
Citizens who have not yet evacuated
should do nothing rash.
Take care.

There was nobody left to hear it.
Seoul was just about deserted.

Maybe sixty thousand remained.
Flocks of crows, an uncommon sight,
had free run of Seoul

At dawn that day,
a baby
had just been born,
one of the sixty thousand.

As day was breaking,
communist soldiers in fur hats
marched through the streets.

The baby
was crying.
The mother with almost no milk
was holding her fatherless newborn.

It was a birth at which none rejoiced,
but nobody said it was a birth
that should not have happened.
The mother will grow strong.
The baby too will grow stronger, little by little.

VOLUME 20

The Present

Our lovely land of rivers, mountains!

Ah, did we have such hatred that we took revenge?
Did we have such resentment that we took revenge
and again revenge?

Since Liberation, Korea has been a land of blood.
Every single nook and cranny of our whole peninsula
has become a cursed place
where one is forced to kill another.

Ended now a thousand years of warm hearts in every village.

After 1945
suddenly
Jeong-tae turned from a boy into a young men.
You too
are no longer yourself
but your enemy's enemy.

You there, America's enemy? The USSR's enemy?
What country are you a descendant of?

When Jeong-tae had been drinking
he longed to see his right-wing father
then if he drank more
he longed to see his left-wing maternal uncle.
The people who'd loved him
when he was a child.

Seven-year-old Nam-ok

In a roadside shack in Osan
lived a brother and sister whose parents had been killed.
The brother was fifteen, and
– the child below him having died –
then came Nam-ok, seven.

Her brother had gone along the railway lines collecting coals;
she was all alone,
having fun playing marbles.

Their land's sky was completely occupied by American planes.

No Cheon-myeong

'The deer,
a pathetic animal on account of its long neck.'

The woman who wrote that poem,
had a pointed chin,
wore traditional Korean skirt and jacket,
the skirt short, the jacket-ribbons long.

On June 24, 1950,
she was invited for a convivial supper
at the house of the older poet Mo Yun-suk,
who afterward accompanied her home in a jeep.

After the war broke out on June 25,
Mo Yun-suk hid on Aegi Hill behind Ewha Womans University.
She sent someone to No Cheon-myeong to ask for some food
and two summer jackets.

That woman,
far from sending summer jackets, demanded:
Tell me where Mo Yun-suk is.
If you don't
I'll hand you over to the security forces.

Soon loudspeakers echoed over Aegi Hill:
The reactionary Mo Yun-suk is hiding on this mountain.
Report her on sight.

In an extreme situation people have to betray even friends and
        colleagues.
In an extreme situation even lyric poets
become cold-blooded enemies.
In an extreme situation a delicate spinster
becomes a cruel witch.
In an extreme situation a simple rural emotion becomes an evil
        ideology.

When Seoul was recaptured, No Cheon-myeong was sentenced to
        death.
That was commuted to a life sentence,
then reduced to twenty years,
and soon
she was released on bail after writers sent in a petition.
Dressed in a white jacket and black skirt, No Cheon-myeong
turned up at a meeting of woman-writers in ruined Myeong-dong.

A Chance Encounter

Allied search teams were in full swing.
Enemy search teams also.

Somewhere near Palgong Mountain
Jeong Hae-bong,

a member of the twelfth regiment's search team,
encountered Jeong Hae-seon, from the enemy search team.

They stood there, ten yards apart,
aiming rifles at each other.
Then one exclaimed:
'Brother!'
The other replied:
'Is that you, Hae-seon?'
They fell into each other's arms.
The elder was twenty,
the younger eighteen.

Jeong Hae-seon joined the Southern search unit.
The two brothers, Jeong Hae-bong
and Jeong Hae-seon
both ate a lot of rice.
Rice was their hometown, their parents..

Eon-nyeon in Siberia

In the 1920s
some Koreans
made their way beyond Mongolia
into Russia,
journeyed all the way to near Lake Baikal
and settled in a ruined hut kept standing by props.

Such a long way to go to live.

Despite blizzards
and days so cold their urine froze,
they managed
not to freeze to death.

So harsh a way to live.

One freezing morning
a girl in Korean dress, long skirt and blouse,
a water pot on her head
went to fetch water
carrying a club to smash the ice

Not yet called Anna or Tatiana,
just Eon-nyeon, Pretty Girl.

Her father had not come back home for several days.
Boarding a sledge,
he went off to a hunting-lodge
in Bear Forest

Eon-nyeon had
two younger brothers
and two younger sisters

The family had grown as they journeyed on.

They're not yet called Sergei or Josip or Boris but
First Twin
Second Twin
Dong-seop
Geut-seop
Below Eon-nyeon
Little Girl
Last Girl

Once she turned eight Eon-nyeon became an adult.
She had been living the days
she was destined to live.

Seong-jin

The Japanese imposed the solar calendar on the Korean people.

They abolished the first Korean festival,
the first day of the first lunar month,
Lunar New Year –
New Year ancestral offerings they abolished too.

January 1, solar new year, was the Japanese New Year.
Unknown to the authorities
we celebrated our own New Year.

Lunar New Year was our Independence Movement.

Broiled beef
fried flat cakes
cinnamon punch afloat with thin flakes of ice
boiled rice
steamed fish

Wearing new clothes we went round paying our respects.
But Seong-jin's family in their grass hut outside the village
kept neither the Korean New Year
nor the Japanese New Year.

You would find there no bright party clothes,
no rice cakes.
Unearthing the root of an arrowroot vine
from the sunny side of some hill
Seong-Jin would chew hard on the root
for sudden new energy.

On a New Year's morning
his prick stood erect in vain.
In June that year the war began.

One month later, when the People's Army was in charge for three
        months,
he served as illiterate chairman for the Democratic Young People's
        Front
after which he went missing, permanently.

Hallelujah

Outside Ganghwa town on Ganghwa Island
there's Gapgot Point, a place where breezes blow.
In the fields of Gapgot,
once the distinctive February wind drops off,
the March wind comes along.
Skylarks venturing upward are hurt by the wind.

Across the whirlwind-stirred sea,
in the haze of the Gimpo plains
the April wind urges young rice seed-beds to sprout.

The seedlings are planted out in May.
As people plant the rice, they shout:
Hallelujah
Hallelujah

Once Christianity arrived at isolated villages
believers
and non-believers
became deadly foes.

In a single village
Baptists and Episcopalians
each the others' foes
could not intermarry
or attend each others' wedding parties.

A member of the Holiness Church, Gwak Il-gyu,
who shouts Hallelujah a hundred times a day,
is getting married to Hong Sun-ja of the same church,
who shouts Hallelujah two hundred times a day.

Episcopalians dare not attend
the wedding.
Even if they're cousins
or distant relatives.

Former co-workers,
former close friends and kin
vanished,
became one another's foes.

The moment the North Korea armies arrived
those on the left arose and killed those of the right.
Once the North withdrew
the right was left
having slaughtered all those of the left.

The churches prospered.
The churches distributed
American relief food and goods.
People came flocking
to collect wheat flour.
They even received a second-hand suit of clothes.

All were forced to shout Hallelujah!
Out in the fields at harvest time too:
Hallelujah!
Hallelujah!

Ji Ha-ryeon

At the height of Japanese rule the blue sky begot despair.
She was a poet's wife,
a poet's comrade.
From the very start her belated love
was heading for open-eyed darkness.

When she published her short story 'Farewell' in the review *Munjang*
in 1940, in the midst of the Sino-Japanese War
and just before the Pacific War,
colonised Korea
was proud of its camellia-like woman writer,
Ji Ha-ryeon.

She was Masan's drunken spirit,
the desire of the night sea in Masan Bay.

Lovely Ji Ha-ryeon fell in love with handsome Im Hwa's
        tuberculosis.
She made a secret conversion.
Poet Im Hwa's original name was Yi Hyeon-uk.

They had the happiest times after Liberation.
Her husband,
putting on light linen clothes,
invited Kim Sun-nam
and Ham Se-deok to dinner,
a meal which his wife in her apron prepared to perfection.

They joined the underground,
went North.

Just after the war, the poet was executed,
the poet's wife
was thrown into an asylum.
She spent days of despair, raving and fainting,
then died like trash.

Ideology, that was their dream.
Ideology, that was their death.
Ji Ha-ryeon.

Literature, revolution, love
beneath skies that spout blue blood.

Lieutenant Bak Baek

Lieutenant Bak Baek,
adjutant of the search company, 2nd battalion, 16th regiment, 8th
       division.

He advanced as far as Chosan
on the banks of the Yalu River. He was very much moved,
       impassioned.
It was early winter, 1950.
He gazed across the river
at Manchuria, Chinese land.

They encountered the Communist Chinese army.
His body turned into a hedgehog.
On a hill
between Huicheon and Gujang
he was taken prisoner by the Chinese army.

The company commander was killed in action,
two soldiers were killed, three injured,
and the remaining thirty taken prisoner.

The POW camp at Gwansan in Hwapung
held five hundred South Korean soldiers
and three hundred American soldiers.
In the bitter winter prisoners kept dying.

In the camp
each room held twenty men, no space to lie down.
If one died,
the rest had a little more space.

Keeping prisoners' corpses
for two or three days in the room,
leaning them against the wall
at roll-call,
the rest shared the rations of the dead.

They were given one handful of corn twice a day.
In one day fifty or so died.
One cupful of lice came crawling
from every corpse.
Some died gnawing icicles.
Numb from frostbite,
they felt no pain when a finger was cut off.

Lieutenant Bak Baek did not die. He came back in an exchange of
       prisoners.

Bracken in Namdaemun's Dokkaebi Market

Goods from the PX on the American base at Yongsan are loaded
       onto a truck.
Kim Cheol-su, a Korean,
and Harry, a black American,
are expert thieves.

They pass the checkpoint at the back gate
when MP John Beckham is on duty,
that's 4.30 in the morning.

At 5.30
they deliver to Pyo Jong-seon in Namdaemun's Dokkaebi Market.

Watches,
chocolate,
'Akadama' cigarettes,
Camels,
blankets,
military boots,
UN jackets,
fountain pens,
woollen underwear,
gum,
electric razors.

Pyo Jong-seon is from Haeju, up in Hwanghae province.
He never haggles over goods.
He pays what they ask.
This makes him popular,
So the thieves
sell to him cheap.

His nickname is Bracken of Mount Suyang.
On Mount Suyang in Haeju
there's a shrine commemorating
the Chinese brothers Boyi and Shuqi.

When Mount Suyang Bracken
goes home,
he tells his first grand-daughter about Simcheong,
the second one about Princess Nangnang.

He was one of the rich folk of Chungmu-ro street
but one day
American MPs, preceded by Korean MPs,
raided his store and took him away.

Yi Jung-seop

In 1952
people were drinking Nakdong River *soju*.
In a bar in an alley of Hyangchon-dong in Daegu
Yi Jung-seop vomited.
Colonel Yi Gi-ryeon
jokingly mocked the drunken Yi Jung-seop:
'Hey! You smell like a proletarian!'

That means
you're a commie, you're a red.

The next day Yi Jong-seop, having sobered up,
remembered the words about his proletarian smell.
He remembered them the day after,
and the next day, as well.
His whole body shrank.

He went to see the head of investigations in Daegu police station.

'I am not a red.
Please certify
that I'm not a red.'

His friend the poet Ku Sang came to take him home.
Everywhere people were suffering from red persecution complexes.
If someone says
you're a red, you're done.
If someone reports you as a red, you're done.
Such was the age. Fearful.

I am not a red.

Two Men

September 29, 1950.

The day before, the three months of communist rule had ended.
The Republic of Korea that had run away
came back.

The city was still empty.

At the Gwanhwamun intersection
one man came limping from Jong-ro 1-ga.
A ragged figure was approaching
along Sinmun-ro.

They met in the middle of the intersection. They were strangers
        to each other.

For a full thirty minutes
they talked.
They told tales
and listened to tales
about how each had survived,
survived in hiding.

How painful it was to live alone,
how despondent they felt
to have survived alone.

The two men shared a cigarette, then parted, saying: 'See you
        again.'

Midday came.
At the intersection,
not so much as a mouse in sight.

Na Jeong-gu of Myeong-dong

Anyone was free to get drunk and collapse in ruined Myeong-dong,
free to piss to his heart's content
on the eulalia growing as dense as pubic hair
between the pieces of broken brick
and cement walls.
Anyone was free to show off,
bragging how splendid he'd once been
but now he was a beggar.
Anyone was free to become an artist
the moment he stood beside an artist.

Beside the tall painter Kim Hwan-gi
anyone could turn into a modern artist
who painted pictures of Joseon-era white jars.
Beside Kim Hyang-an, the former wife of poet Yi Sang,
now the wife of Kim Hwan-gi,
anyone could turn into a stylish essayist.
While walking along with chain-smoking Yi Myeong-on,
anyone could turn into an essayist and former journalist.

Poet Bak In-hwan died
after writing his boisterous poem 'The Rocking Horse and the Lady,
        Virginia Woolf'.
Anyone who shook hands with Kim Su-yeong,
who had joined the volunteer army
and was just out of Geoje Island POW camp,
became a post-war poet.

In ruined Myeong-dong there was the freedom of the True and False
        as one.

The drunkard Na Jeong-gu,
who pushed his way in wherever people were drinking,
was today a poet,
tomorrow an essayist.
What might he be the day after?

So long as he had a mouth to drink with
he was free to enter the bars Poem or Eunjeong
and join any group he found there.

Ah, in the ruins of Myeong-dong under the Republic of Korea
there was freedom for every kind of extravagance and bluff,
freedom hanging in the air like the spell of a dead age.

Hong Sa-jun

One writer's dream was glorious, his life short.
Hong Sa-jun,
a fine-featured young man,
was a literary star
during the three months of the communist occupation.

North Korean writers praised him highly.

Young Hong Sa-jun's novel *The Deer*
was idolised as a model of proletarian literature.
Writers who came down to Seoul
such as An Hui-nam,
Yi Won-jo,
Yi Gi-yeong,
Bak Tae-won encouraged him, one after another.
On their recommendation
he enjoyed the honor of visiting Pyongyang.

In August 1950
he returned from his visit to Pyongyang.
He turned from being a leftist to a rightist.
Pyongyang had disillusioned him.

I am a rightist.
I saw the reality of Pyongyang.
Tell everyone
that I am a rightist.
I curse what lies beyond the 38th parallel.

After Seoul was recaptured he was arrested as a traitor.
To save him, the writer Kim Dong-ni
visited the police and the prosecutors.
When Hong Sa-jun was imprisoned,
fearful, apprehensive,
he resolved to escape.

While attempting to escape he was killed. He was like a drop of dew.

If he had only held on a little longer,
he would have been released
after investigation.
His writing would have bloomed to the fullest.
After all, the poet No Cheon-myeong, who ran wild under the
          communists,
she was released.

Gwon Jin-gyu

His Japanese wife died.
Love lost.

Alone he moulded clay
chiseled stone.

The sculptor Gwon Jin-gyu
had a room in Donam-dong, Seoul.

The sculptures were quite at home.
The sculptor
was a guest squatting on the edge of a camp bed in a corner.

One clay figure breathing.
One sculptor gasping.

It seems there are cliffs in art.
Failing to avoid the cliff,
he walked over the edge
and after that, there was nothing.

He ended his life.
Not because he hated the world
Not because he hated himself.

Because art had been driven out.

Lovers

In the winter of 1953
Jiri Mountain was the main objective.
The path to Jiri Mountain crosses many steep mountains.
The Imsil contingent found itself scattered all over the ridges
when it got cut off from the main battleline.
News came that the guerilla unit in Huimun Mountain had been
      annihilated.
Feet were heavy as they marched on by night.
The Jiri Mountain contingent
were sure to be attacked by the expeditionary forces.
Where could the sixth division of the 102nd guards' battalion be?
They too must have been attacked.

Each evening they cut arrowroot vines and plaited shelters,
with pine branches to form a roof.

Mount Jang-an was full of expeditionary forces.
Night fell.
Flashlights were moving upward.
The lights of the expeditionary forces.
They ran madly, walked, crawled.
They wedged themselves under rocks.
Nearby
two people were holding their breath and trembling.

In the falling snow
those two were comrades:
a woman member of the contingent, Gang Sun-ok
and a straggler from the People's Army, Jang Gwan-ho.
Where had the other members of the contingent gone?

We've fallen into those bastards' trap.
It would be a waste of energy
to go on wandering.
Let's see what things are like here.

Sleep overcame them.

A loudspeaker rang out from below:
You're surrounded.
Come out quietly with your hands up.
Let yourselves be embraced by the Republic of Korea.

They heard it in their sleep
as day broke.

The two were found lying side by side.
Their hands were blue with frostbite.
Barefoot, for they had taken the wrappings off their feet.
Locked in a tight embrace, they did not move.
Soldiers shook them
but they did not budge.
They had frozen to death in the night.

That girl from the South, Gang Sun-ok,
and the man from the North
must have fallen in love on their march over the mountains.
Loving
then dying,
no rancour remains.

They were not far from the secret hideout.
Unable to make it there
and dying,
no rancour remains.

Im Chang-ho's Death Anniversary

There were almost no young men left in Jeju Island.
They had all been drafted into the army,
or sent to distant coal mines,
or conscripted to fight in the South Sea Islands.

From every seaside village
twenty
or thirty
had gone off *en masse*.

In one village
twenty-five gone off
between the ages of eighteen and thirty left.

The girls left to be comfort women.
Once they left
after a couple of postcards
there was no more news.
At the end of the Japanese occupation,
even the houses were requisitioned for the military,
the harvested grain taken to feed the army.

Those remaining,
between the ages of fourteen
and seventy were mobilised.
In the days of forced labour
one or two hundred
were forced to work in canteens.

When Japan surrendered,
some three hundred corpses
were piled up at the workplaces.
Such was Liberation.
Such was Jeju Island at Liberation.

Half the young folk who had been taken away
didn't come back.
Those who came back
were injured,
were invalids.
A few lights floated on the sea at night
from boats fishing for hairtail.

Im Gyeong-bok
of Bonggae-dong in the hilly regions of Jeju Island
could not find the body of his father Im Chang-ho.
He searched three different forced-labour camps
but could not locate his father's body
among the corpses.

Weeping bitterly
he burned a set of his father's clothes
and put the ashes
into the grave mound for his father.
That was on August 17, 1945,
two days after Liberation.

He chose August 15,
Liberation Day,
as his father's death anniversary day.

'Father!
Father!'
Returning home
after building the grave mound
he called out toward the horizon.
'Father!'
That night in a dream
his father came back in a boat.

The Lady Eom

Queen Min, who stood up to the Daewon-gun, her father-in-law,
was a fearsome woman.
On the faces of the court ladies
who slept with her husband King Gojong
she inflicted all kinds of scars,
and added all kinds of harsh punishments.
She was murdered one night by a band of Japanese thugs.
Her dead body was burned,
became a handful of bones
that someone secretly buried.

Later, the Lady Eom,
who had kept her distance from Queen Min, was called
to be the recipient of Gojong's love.

Lady Eom was benevolent.
The courtiers felt relieved at last.

This wise queen,
separately from the schools of the foreign missionaries
founded Yanjeong School,
Jinmyeong Ladies' School,
Sukmyeong Ladies' School with money from the privy purse
and her own resources.

Yangjeong School offered traditional education,
Jinmyeong and Sukmyeong aimed at modern education.

In the end her son Eun, known as King Yeongchin,
was sent away to Japan as a hostage at the age of eleven.
His royal father
and royal mother were broken-hearted.
His royal father
inscribed for him the character 忍 'endure'.
His mother, the Lady Eom, died of typhoid fever
before ever seeing again the Crown Prince, her only son.

Yi Hae-myeong's Wife

During the war, people were less than animals.
During the war,
they were insects, they were netted fish.
They wriggled
they flapped, they collapsed, grew stiff.
People were as vulgar as vulgar could be.

On March 5, 1951,
people went into air-raid shelters
and shook with fear of being bombed.
At the least sound of a plane
cold sweat ran down their backs.
Once the sound of the plane had died away
vegetables came out, meat appeared,
rice-cakes too appeared
in front of the Central Cinema at Wangsim-ni.

They had to go on living amidst the bombs.
They had to buy and sell.
If a bomb fell somewhere close,
the merchants vanished
leaving their bundles of cabbages where they were.

In March the Chinese forces began to retreat.
On March 10 the People's Army withdrew.

Yi Hae-myeong, from the royal line of Joseon,
was forced to go with the People's Army as a volunteer.

In streets littered with corpses
Yi Hae-myeong's wife
wore men's underwear
and came out to sell women's clothes.
She never hid during bombing raids
but stayed in her market corner

Even when she'd had nothing to eat for three days
her face retained its human dignity,
female modesty too,
and her woman's patience
remained alive, enduring the pain deep inside her.

In a rough age
she remained, still a human being.

DDT

Soon after Liberation in 1945,
Seoul began to swarm with 370 different political parties and civic
    groups.
Every morning when you woke up
several more had hung out their signboards.
Parties of just five members appeared, without even a signboard.

The commander of the occupying forces, General Hodge,
detested the Koreans, calling them cats or worse.
All the Koreans working in Hodge's headquarters
and the Koreans in the streets
outside his headquarters
were liberally doused in DDT.
Smothered in that poisonous powder
the Koreans would giggle helplessly
while seething with shame.

Thanks to the Americans who came for the war
in 1950 Korea again became a land of DDT.
Fleas, bugs and the plentiful lice and nits about their bodies,
even the invisible microbes,
were uncivilised
so the Americans drenched the Koreans
in plentiful quantities of DDT.

All the orphans likewise
received baptisms in Hallelujah and DDT.
Offspring with neither dad nor mom became the offspring of DDT.

Choi Johan, a war orphan,
had as his family name that of the director of his orphanage, Zion
          Home,
and as his given name
the John of the Gospel of St. John.
His original name, Bak Seon-sik was completely forgotten.

Since his room happened to be next to a stinking cesspool,
Choi Johan's blanket
always smelt of a mixture of sewage and DDT.

Ah, home, sweet home.

Yi Jeong-i's family

They walked all the way from Jinnampo in North Korea
to Hongseong in South Korea's Chungcheong province.
They walked and walked.
For twenty days they fled.

Yi Jeon-hae
and her sister Yi Jeong-i
with their parents following them.

All day long walking with nothing to eat.
When they found a well
they drank then walked on in the flesh-biting cold.

They dreaded the American troops
so they smeared their clothes
with their own shit.

They spread soot from kitchen chimneys
over their faces.
The mother became
a beggar-mum,
her daughters beggar kids

Their bodies stank of shit.
Instead of American troops, dogs came running.

Their robust father
likewise
blackened his face. The teeth inside his lips looked stronger still.

When snow fell
they ventured into a village
and were saved by a shed
or an empty cowstall.

Three hundred miles they walked
to arrive at Hongseong, and settle there.

When China attacked in January 1951,
Chinese forces never reached Hongseong,
being held back near the 38th parallel.
The family began a new life amidst the hills and fields of Hongseong,
purchased a big hospital.

One daughter, Yi Jeong-i, got married,
became the wife of poet-professor Kim Young-moo. Never late for
        Mass.

mpty House

In Jangsa-dong, central Seoul, a big tiled-roof house lay empty.
After Seoul was recaptured for the second time
someone, intent on taking over the house,
came along, snarling:

'This house used to be a red's; from now on it's mine.'

Another man came along, snarling:

'I must live here.
A red killed my brother.'

Yet another man came along, accompanied by an MP.

'I'm anti-communist fighter Bak Jong-sik, don't you know?
You two, get out.
This house should belong to an anti-communist fighter.
Down with Kim Il-sung!
Defeat the communist party!'

Bak Jong-sik, a relative of the MP, took over the house.
After the MP left in his jeep,
the new owner moved into the empty house.
He removed the spider webs.
He had a name-plate made.
He bought a fierce dog.

'Beware of the dog!' was painted on the gate.